How to

Outsta   g

Nursery Leader

OTHER TITLES FROM BLOOMSBURY EDUCATION

How to be an Outstanding Childminder
by Allison Lee

How to be an Outstanding Early Years Practitioner
by Louise Burnham

*How to be an Outstanding Primary School Teacher,
Second Edition*
by David Dunn

How to be an Outstanding Primary Teaching Assistant
by Emma Davie

How to be an Outstanding Primary Middle Leader
by Zoë Paramour

How to be an Outstanding Nursery Leader

Allison Lee

BLOOMSBURY EDUCATION
LONDON OXFORD NEW YORK NEW DELHI SYDNEY

BLOOMSBURY EDUCATION
Bloomsbury Publishing Plc
50 Bedford Square, London, WC1B 3DP, UK

BLOOMSBURY, BLOOMSBURY EDUCATION and the Diana logo are trademarks
of Bloomsbury Publishing Plc

First published in Great Britain 2018

A catalogue record for this book is available from the British Library.

ISBN: PB: 978-1-4729-5257-8; ePDF: 978-1-4729-5258-5;
ePub: 978-1-4729-5259-2

2 4 6 8 10 9 7 5 3 1 (paperback)

Typeset by Newgen KnowledgeWorks Pvt. Ltd., Chennai, India
Printed and bound by CPI Group (UK) Ltd., Croydon, CR0 4YY

MIX
Paper from
responsible sources
FSC® C013604

To find out more about our authors and books visit www.bloomsbury.com
and sign up for our newsletters.

Contents

Acknowledgements

Since starting work in the childcare profession some 25 years ago, I have been privileged to work with a large number of families, all of whom have given me the opportunity of being part of their child's life. My career has also put me in contact with many professionals who have shared their knowledge, experience and expertise, enabling me to enhance the provision provided in my own settings.

Special thanks, however, go to the staff teams, past and present, who have provided me with the foundation and support required to build the exceptional childcare provisions I am now proud to own. I would like to thank each and every one of you for your outstanding contribution to childcare.

Introduction

No manager of a childcare setting should set their sights low. 'Outstanding' is achievable and is the only grade a manager should be looking to gain – anything less is simply not good enough!

However, in order to achieve 'outstanding' and, more importantly, to retain this grade, the manager will need to set some firm ground rules and build a knowledgeable and supportive team around them. This takes time, patience and perseverance.

The outstanding manager will need to know every member of their team well; they will need to learn what makes them tick, what their aspirations are and how they can help steer the team to outstanding status.

The outstanding manager needs to learn the art of listening to, delegating, guiding and motivating the team all day, every day. There will be no place for complacency, and each and every member of the team needs to understand the importance of the role they play.

There are two very different sets of values to take into account when managing a childcare setting:

- the value of good childcare practice
- the value of good management.

Both of the above aspects are equally important and neither is negotiable.

I hope this book is a useful guide for all managers of childcare settings, whether looking for advice on building a team, dealing with staffing problems, promoting your business or simply wanting up-to-date guidance on everyday issues.

Printable versions of all the template forms and documents provided in the book are available online at www.bloomsbury.com/outstanding-nursery-leader. Note that these versions are editable and you should adapt them to suit the requirements of your setting before using them.

Chapter 1
The outstanding nursery manager in a nutshell

Making a nursery outstanding is all about teamwork. No manager can bring a nursery to the outstanding stage without a hard-working, knowledgeable and dedicated team behind them. However, the manager themselves needs to be in control; they need to know their team well, be aware of any potential pitfalls and steer their team in the right direction. There will be times when it feels like an uphill struggle, when staff may seem they are pulling apart instead of together; but when the main goal appears to be elusive, this is when the outstanding manager will show their true colours. Bringing calm when there is chaos, looking at problems logically and putting everyday issues into perspective are all part of a manager's everyday duties; however, doing this well, without drama or excuses, will make all the difference.

Let us think about what makes someone a leader. Take some time out to truly think about your own qualities. Ask yourself why you want to become a manager, then ask yourself what makes a good leader and what sets apart a good leader from an outstanding leader. Is this something that you can personally achieve?

It is important, from the outset, to understand your own qualities and to be honest with yourself when deciding which areas you need to improve on. You need to know what kind of leader you think you might *currently* make and then consider how you are going to become the leader you *want* to be – the leader that your team *needs*.

In addition to a nursery having a strong manager, it is essential that strong leadership is found at all levels of the organisation, including owners, room supervisors and seniors.

All practitioners should have a shared primary purpose and that purpose should involve providing the best possible care and opportunities for children to be happy and to achieve. Having a starting point, or shared primary purpose, will encourage the whole team to focus on the job in hand and work together to achieve the desired outcome.

Exercise

Make a list of all the staff currently in your team and then prioritise them in areas of expertise. Add their strengths and weaknesses and then analyse ways in which you could help them to improve their performance. For example, could they benefit from additional training or would it be worthwhile letting them shadow a more experienced member of staff?

What makes an outstanding leader?

Outstanding leaders have many different guises. In order to run an outstanding practice, nursery managers will often be required to take on different roles to lead their staff and deal with specific situations or challenges as and when they arise. Let's take a look at some of these.

The role model

It is essential that the manager is a good role model at all times. Being professional is paramount. The manager of any outstanding nursery will be professional all day, every day. It is good to have a friendly and approachable nature so that staff can speak openly and truthfully, but you must remain impartial and professional. It can be hard to maintain a high degree of professionalism day in day out, and sometimes you may feel like sitting back and turning a blind eye when staff appear to be chatting instead of carrying out their duties, but this is asking for trouble – remember, if you allow it once, you will be expected to turn a blind eye all the time!

Being a consistently good role model takes dedication but, in time, setting a good example will, and should, come naturally.

The mediator

At times you may wonder who are the children and who are the staff! There will be times when staff have fallouts and disagreements – after all, they don't usually choose who they work with and they are expected to work as a team for long hours. Your role as a mediator *will* be called upon, of that there is no doubt. Always remain impartial. Listen to both sides of any disagreement but do not escalate the problem. It is the job of the manager to solve problems as quickly and as professionally (that important word again!) as possible. Staff fallouts should never be permitted to surface in front of children or parents – a bickering workforce will most definitely give the wrong impression.

The counsellor

Your team may be incredible and rarely have disagreements but this doesn't mean that they will not have problems outside of the workplace that could potentially impact on their work. They may have relationship problems or financial issues, for example, which they decide to confide in you about. You will need to deal with these issues confidentially. Whilst personal problems are often seen as being separate from work, it is inevitable that they will impact on how staff are feeling and therefore operating in the workplace, and it is better for the manager to be aware of these problems so any potential issues can be dealt with in a professional and discreet manner to avoid impacting on the service you are providing.

The teacher

You may have a variety of people in your team, from apprentices to degree-qualified practitioners, and each member of the team will need to be 'taught' the nursery's procedures on a level that suits them, whilst upholding the high level of service the setting demands. Nurseries will have their own policies and procedures, in addition to the essential legislation they are required to follow, and relevant information needs to be cascaded to staff accordingly. The team needs to be confident in carrying out observations and assessments for example, and staff must be secure in their knowledge of the nursery's procedures and routines in order to do their job to the best of their ability. You may be required to attend training courses and cascade relevant information to staff, and you will need to be confident doing this in an easy-to-understand way so that staff at all levels understand what is required.

The friend

It is debatable whether a manager can be a friend to their team but this needn't be a problem. If we look at what being a 'friend' means, there is, in my opinion, no problem with being a manager and a friend to your staff. A friend is everything an outstanding manager should be – a good listener, impartial, helpful, kind and considerate – and there is absolutely no reason why you cannot be all of these things in the workplace. I would however advise caution when socialising outside of work and make sure that the two roles are kept separate. Work should not be discussed when socialising and socialising should not be discussed in the workplace. Remember the need to be a role model – this can and must be maintained at all times in the workplace, but will it be as easy to do at a colleague's 21st birthday party? If the answer is 'no' I would advise you to steer clear of the party!

Social media can also be a downfall. When staff send you a 'friend request' on Facebook, should you accept? There are two sides of looking at this. If you accept, you are equipped with the knowledge of what your staff get up to in their spare time, but equally they can see the messages that you post. This shouldn't be a problem if you remain professional when using social media but you need to think about how you will deal with inappropriate postings from staff. A clear policy on social media should deal with this effectively but, as a manager, you may need to issue 'gentle reminders' of what is and is not acceptable.

The boss

A nursery manager, or indeed any manager, will not get the best from their team if they try to rule with an iron rod. A manager needs to be firm but fair. If you do not listen to your team, they will stop making suggestions; if they stop making suggestions, your nursery will not improve; if improvements are not made, the workplace will become boring and staid. This is a vicious cycle and not one that an outstanding nursery evolves from. You are in charge and you have all the responsibilities that this brings with it but you are not alone. You have, hopefully, a strong team around you, who all want the same end result. It is therefore paramount that you listen to your team and accept each and every one of them for the merits that they bring to the workplace. Use their skills and expertise and work with them on their weaker points, and you will not need to be an ogre!

Essential skills needed by managers

To be an outstanding manager in a childcare setting you will need to be able to draw on a wide range of professional and personal skills to be able to steer the business in the correct way, lead an outstanding team and provide the best possible service to those using the setting. In order to do all this you will need the following essential skills:

- confidence
- assertiveness
- sense of humour
- staying power
- acceptance
- responsibility
- accountability
- vision
- honesty
- flexibility.

Let us now look at each of the above and discuss why these particular skills are essential for managers to have in a childcare setting.

Confidence
Managers need to have confidence in their own abilities in order to effectively lead and manage a team. In order to be able to influence the behaviour of others and lead a team towards a shared goal, the manager will need to understand the importance of being proactive and have the ability to develop and shape the way the team thinks and operates.

Assertiveness

Whilst it is not the primary role of the manager to simply act as a 'trouble-shooter', it is important for the manager to have good self-esteem and be assertive in their role as a leader. Assertiveness often comes hand-in-hand with confidence. The more confident a person feels, the more likely they are to be assertive and to gain the respect of the team. Being 'assertive' should not be confused with being 'aggressive'. It is worth remembering that it is possible to be assertive whilst being open to the views and ideas of others, and this is something an outstanding manager will keep in mind.

In order to be assertive you should decide what you would like to happen, ask yourself if this is fair and possible, remain calm, express your feelings openly and give praise when it is due, whilst being open to criticism.

Sense of humour

This is an essential skill in many job roles but none more so than when working with children. Whatever is happening in the workplace, it pays to remember that children are present and they should never be witness to raised voices or angry altercations. Always deal with potential problems away from the children and remember, even if you are having a bad day, it costs nothing to smile, and smiling often results in us feeling better!

Staying power

If the manager walks out at the first sign of a problem then the team will inevitably fall apart and the setting will never achieve the outstanding grade they are aiming for. Difficult situations should be viewed not as 'obstacles' but as 'stepping stones' to a stronger, brighter and ultimately more successful future. By tackling a problem confidently and working through difficulties logically you will do wonders for your self-esteem and boost your confidence.

Acceptance

Sometimes we have to accept that situations cannot be altered. You may have tried your best but still have been faced with an upset parent, for example. It is important to remember that none of us are perfect and we cannot please all of the people, all of the time. An outstanding manager will accept praise and compliments when they are due, whilst acknowledging imperfection and understanding that everyone makes mistakes from time to time. By accepting mistakes, and learning from them, we can develop professional practice rather than dwelling on what went wrong and why. Effective managers must accept that their team is not perfect but, equally importantly, they need to accept that they themselves are not perfect either!

Responsibility

Whilst it has to be remembered that the manager is ultimately responsible for the overall running of the setting, it is also true to say that the rest of the team can, and should, be on hand to *support* the manager. It is important for managers to promote a shared responsibility in the setting and, whilst they are there to lead and guide their team, they must not be allowed to shoulder all the responsibility. An outstanding manager will always be alert and notice and respond to situations but they should ensure that their team understand their own roles within the company and be able to delegate tasks accordingly.

Accountability

Everyone in the setting, including the manager, is accountable. A confident manager will never blame someone else for their own mistakes and they will help their team to find solutions to any problems as and when they arise.

Vision

Without a vision the setting will lack clarity. The setting will have no clear aims and objectives and the team will simply plod on doing what they have always done with no real understanding as to why. Having a vision sets a clear future along a positive and imaginative path. It provides a shared goal for the team and gives reason and importance to the work currently being done whilst setting out what it aims to achieve in the future. Having a vision prevents the business from becoming boring and stale and embraces the ideas and shared values of the whole team. Vision instils motivation and pride in a job well done. Managers need to embrace the whole ethos of the setting and its vision in order to encourage and motivate their team into understanding why they do what they do and so help them to see the value in their own work.

Honesty

Being reflective is all about looking at our own role and considering whether we could have done things differently and, if we had, might a situation have been improved. In order to be reflective it is essential to be honest, and managers who have experienced difficult situations and have been able to reflect on their own role with honesty will be able to learn and develop their own practice. Reflection can at times be daunting and intimidating, especially if it is apparent that we have not acted in a fair way, but this kind of situation can be an invaluable learning experience and should be seen as such.

Flexibility

When reflecting on our own roles it is essential that we are open to change. There is little point in reflecting on our own practice if we are not willing to be flexible in our thinking and actions. After reflecting on our own practice we may have discovered things that we could have done differently, but unless we are open to personal change and flexible in our thinking this will never be achieved.

Leadership styles

Now that you know the characteristics of what makes a good leader, it is time to look at leadership *styles.* Some people are 'natural leaders' born to the role, whilst others need to learn how to lead a team. There is no right or wrong way to 'lead' as long as the end result is the desired one. When adopting a particular leadership style you should focus on your own natural strengths and then learn how to gain in confidence in other areas and skills that are not automatically natural to you. Our own personal experiences will help us to adopt a specific style of leadership. You may, for example, think back favourably on time spent at school, college or university, having had a positive experience of a particular teacher, and would like to follow in their footsteps in your own leadership style. Alternatively, a negative experience will help you to understand what you do not wish to repeat.

Some of the main leadership styles are:

- **The democratic leader** – who takes into account the ideas and views of the team and values those who work within the team. This kind of leader allows practitioners to take 'ownership' of their role by allowing input into documents and procedures. The drawback of this is when the staff team may not have sufficient knowledge to make an informed decision or give knowledgeable advice or feedback.

- **The visionary leader** – who knows what they want and how to go about getting it. This kind of leader is energetic and enthusiastic and usually has a goal to work towards. The drawback of this type of leadership is when the leader has limited knowledge and fails to realise that those working with them are more experienced than they are or if the goal they have set is unrealistic.

- **The pace-setting leader** – who is similar to the visionary leader in that they are energetic and enthusiastic with a focus on meeting goals. The drawback might be confusion and lack of morale for practitioners who struggle to keep the pace whilst carrying out their own day-to-day duties.

- **The united leader** – who likes harmony within the workforce and is adept at motivation. However, whilst supporting staff and reducing tension is always a good thing, this should never take the place of good practice, and the negative side of being a united leader could be the inability or unwillingness to tackle poor practice, resulting in a leader with no direction or purpose.

- **The controlling leader** – who gives orders and expects results without question or discussion. Whilst this can be a good way to lead when an urgent decision is required, it is not an effective long-term way to lead a team. The controlling leader uses shock tactics, which will not engage or motivate the team, and may even result in the total opposite happening when staff purposely choose to defy the controller.

- **The pedagogical leader** – who knows the sector. They will undoubtedly have experience and be capable of leading and teaching their team. They will understand the dynamics of change within the early years sector and know how pedagogical principles are embedded in the early years framework. Children will be at the heart of everything they do.

It is apparent that *all* leadership styles have something to offer. Whilst some styles are undoubtedly better than others, it is true to say that leadership requires variety. A good leader identifies what needs to change, whilst an outstanding leader knows how to engage their team in order to make these changes and understands that every member of their team is different and will therefore require an approach that is unique to them.

Whatever style of leader you fall into there is one thing for certain: *all* leaders need to know their subject. You must be knowledgeable in all areas of child development and understand the ways in which children learn. You need to be passionate about your job, be well read, open-minded and willing to stretch and challenge yourself in order to be the best that you can be. Having said that, an outstanding manager should also realise that they cannot know everything there is to know and, whilst it is important that they are well read and confident in their field, there will always be something more to learn. Situations will arise that challenge your way of thinking and it is important that you have a thirst for, and embrace, new and exciting challenges.

Exercise

After looking at the different types of leaders, consider where your own leadership style lies. Is this the kind of leader you envisage yourself to be or do you need to make some changes to your own style?

Theories behind effective leadership

Leadership theories have been studied for decades but in principle they fall into the following main categories:

- **The great man theory (1840s)** – this theory was based, without any scientific certainty, on the widely accepted assumption that only a man could possess the characteristics that make a leader. This theory assumed that the qualities required of a great leader were innate and therefore it was believed that leaders were born rather than created.

- **The trait theory (1930s to 40s)** – this theory was based on the belief that leaders could either be born or created. It was understood that leaders possessed certain qualities, such as creativity, a sense of responsibility and great intelligence. The main focus of the trait theory of leadership was on the mental, physical and social characteristics but it was greatly flawed and based on unreliable studies.

- **The behavioural theories (1940s to 50s)** – moving away from the trait theory, the behavioural theories concentrated on the behaviours of leaders, rather than their mental, physical or social characteristics, and challenge the great man theory that leaders are born. The behavioural theories offered the perspective that, with the right conditioning, anyone could be a gifted and natural leader.

- **The contingency theories (1960s)** – the argument behind these theories is that there is no single way to lead and that leadership styles should be pertinent to the situation. The general understanding of the contingency theories is that leaders are more likely to be confident leading when the team involved is responsive.

- **The transactional theories (1970s)** – the transactional theories are also known as exchange theories of leadership and place the emphasis on a positive and mutually beneficial relationship between the leader and those they are leading. For this kind of theory to be effective, rewards or punishments are put in place in order to ensure that the individual and the organisation are working in complete harmony.

- **The transformational theories (1970s)** – this type of leadership theory focuses on the leader building a solid relationship, based on trust, with those around them, which results in an increase in motivation and pride. The leader's charisma and inspiration are used to guide and create a sense of purpose and belonging.

After looking at the different leadership theories, it becomes apparent that no particular theory is without its flaws. Whilst certain traits, such as charisma, confidence and knowledge, will undoubtedly benefit leaders, these traits alone cannot be relied upon and it is therefore important for managers to look at how leadership theories have evolved and to choose the aspects from each that best suit their own circumstances and the situations they find themselves in.

Time for reflection

As a leader it is important to spend time reflecting on the work that you do. This will help you to decide what you have achieved and what still needs working on. Reflection will give you the chance to understand what you do well and encourage you to look at your knowledge, experience and personal attributes in order to understand how you can improve your own performance and ultimately lead your team towards its shared goal.

Finding time to reflect can be difficult, especially given the nature of the business you are in when children, staff and parents are constantly needing your attention. However, it is very important that you regularly take a few minutes to reflect on your own practice. A notebook containing your thoughts and ideas is a useful place to start. Jot down things that have particularly struck you during the day – these may be pleasant, making you proud of what you do, or challenging, making you question the things that you do. Often, challenging aspects of the job help us to put things into perspective and, by making notes to refer back to in the future, you can avoid unnecessary pitfalls and be confident that when a problem does arise you will know how best to deal with it.

When reflecting, try not to focus too heavily on the negatives. Many of us tend to remember only the bad things and this often overshadows all the positive things we have experienced. Putting things into perspective isn't always easy but it is a trait that outstanding leaders will possess. They will be able to see past the anger of a parent who has had to collect their child from the setting due to sickness and understand that the parent isn't blaming anyone for their child's illness – they are simply frustrated at the inconvenience, which may be impacting on their own job. In time the parent's frustration will fade and therefore dwelling on it is pointless.

The reflective leader will be able to identify their own strengths and weaknesses and will be willing to be open and honest with themselves. They will understand their own roles and responsibilities and be able to guide their team to being successful through courage, transparency, passion and vision.

On the whole it is true to say that a good leader is one that inspires and motivates. A good leader should never ask one of their team to do something that they themselves cannot or will not do. Therefore it is important that you are seen to 'walk the floor' and not hide behind a desk in the office. Staff need to know that you know what their job entails and that you can, and will, step in if need be. You should know everyone's job role and be able to carry out everyone's tasks, quite simply because a manager cannot lead a team if they are ignorant to how the setting is run.

Take the time to challenge yourself. Ask yourself why you do certain tasks: are the tasks necessary or are they simply routine? If you don't know why you do something or why you ask a team member to do something then chances are that 'something' is completely unnecessary! Take the time to analyse systems and routines and eliminate those that are unnecessary.

Chapter 2
Building an effective team

I am a firm believer that a team will only ever be as good as its weakest link; therefore the weakest link in an outstanding nursery needs to be pretty strong! So, if a nursery is only as good as its team then the manager has a huge task ahead when selecting the right staff for that team.

Choosing the right staff is probably the most difficult job a manager has to do. Get it right and the new recruit will fit in well and cause you no problems; get it wrong and you may well have a rough ride ahead.

Not only will the right person be knowledgeable and keen but they will also need to fit in with your existing team, and this is not always easy to get right. A candidate may come across very well in an interview, possess all the desired qualifications and have years of knowledge and experience, but if they can't share their knowledge or work in a team securely then chances are they won't bring anything worthwhile to the setting and may well upset the entire dynamics of the existing team.

Advertising for staff

There are a number of ways to advertise for staff, and each brings with it potential benefits and pitfalls. You should think carefully about which might be the best option for your nursery.

- **Newspapers** – advertising vacancies in newspapers targets potential candidates in the local area but it can be very costly. You may get numerous applicants and it can be time-consuming to sift through them.

- **Recruitment agencies** – again these can be costly, but they tend to do most of the legwork for you and will, if requested, only send suitably qualified staff who fit your exact criteria.

- **Social media** – this can be an effective way of advertising vacancies but, like newspaper advertising, you may get a large volume of candidates who will need to be sorted for suitability.

- **Local authority websites** – many local authorities have their own websites for advertising vacancies and these can be very useful and are usually free.

- **Online CV libraries** – these can be very useful as you can categorise your search into areas, experience, qualifications and so forth. The downside of using this type of recruitment is that many people add their CV and forget to remove it when they have found suitable employment or do not update it regularly. This method of recruitment also has a cost implication.

Recruitment

When you have placed your advertisement in whichever way you feel will provide the right calibre of applicant, you will need to wait for the response. It is advisable to put a closing date on your advertisement so that you can plan the interview process and have a date in mind when you hope to fill the vacancy. You may, of course, need to re-advertise at a later date if you do not generate the right response initially.

Once your closing date has arrived you will need to carefully read the CVs and, if you have provided one, application forms of the candidates applying for the job. I would suggest sorting them into three piles as you go: the ones you definitely want to interview, the maybes and the definite nos.

Before making your final interview selection, think again about the vacancy you are trying to fill. It is important to look precisely at the person you need to employ at this particular point in time. If you have a candidate for the position of part-time baby room practitioner who has a vast amount of experience as a supervisor, with a wealth of qualifications and a teaching degree, looking for a full-time position in a pre-school, will they really be the right person to interview? They may sound like the ideal employee and you may well decide to interview them for a different role, but it is important to match the person to the vacancy. Equally, if you have a vacancy for an experienced teacher in your pre-school room, it is pointless expecting a newly qualified level two practitioner to fulfill this role. Careful advertising, which states exactly what you are looking for, should eliminate potential problems like this but it may be that you are looking for someone part time initially with a view to going full time when numbers increase and it is fine to explain this to candidates so they are aware of the hours and role on offer, both currently and in the future.

Many managers have their own methods of interviewing and selecting staff and there is no right or wrong way of doing this. However, what I would say is that it is very important to get a real 'feel' for any potential new employee before offering them a job. Hiring new staff in a nursery has a big impact on the team, the children and the parents and it is therefore very important to be as certain as possible that the decision you are making is the right one.

I would always advise two interviews. The first one can be carried out alone as this will be the time when you verify the person's qualifications, explain the vacancy in more detail and ask the candidate for their background history. This first interview should give you an initial feel for the person. Are they easy to talk to? Do they appear to have the knowledge you require? Are they presentable?

If you are happy at the initial interview stage to invite them back for a second interview, I would suggest carrying out the second interview with your area or deputy manager or, if you have one, the supervisor of the room where the vacancy is available. This will enable you to dig a little deeper and ask more questions about their experience and knowledge, and allow you both to consider the answers you are given. After the second interview you should spend some time with your area or deputy manager, or supervisor, discussing the outcome. You may still be of the opinion that the candidate is suitable but your colleague may have reservations or may have noticed something that you missed, or indeed you yourself may realise at this point that perhaps they are not the right person for the job, particularly if you have interviewed several other people after them.

When you have successfully carried out a first and second interview and are happy that you have found the right person to fit the criteria you are looking for, you will need to contact the person again. At this stage I would recommend explaining that you are considering offering them the position and invite them to ask any questions; they may need the hours clarifying or the pay confirming, for example. It is important at this stage that the candidate is completely certain of what the job entails, the hours, the pay and so forth, as they may be your ideal candidate but you may not be theirs!

If they are accepting of the terms and conditions, the next stage is to invite them for a trial session. This has the benefit of working both for the nursery and for the potential new recruit. Before making any firm decisions you need to know that the person you have interviewed is the right person to join your team, and this can only be done by seeing them in action in the setting. Set aside a suitable time for the candidate to be in the nursery, in the room they will be required to work in if they are offered the position. I would suggest a minimum of three hours and preferably a whole morning or afternoon so that they can get a feel for the nursery's daily procedures and you can see how they adapt to these. It is a good idea to spend some time in the room with them observing how they interact with the children and other staff, but I would also let them spend time without you present and ask your supervisor or deputy manager to observe so that they can see whether anything changes when a manager is not present.

After the trial session spend some time getting feedback. Ask the potential new employee how they felt it went and whether they have enjoyed their time in the nursery. Tell them you will be in touch shortly with a definite decision and then speak to your team. What did they think of him or her? Do they feel they can work with him or her? Was the potential recruit easy to talk to? Did they interact well with the children? Did they ask suitable questions? Were they interested in the nursery? All these questions need to be asked and, more importantly, you need to listen to what you are being told. If a member of staff seems unsure ask them why.

Finally, do a little research of your own. Look at social media and see how they portray themselves. Do you really want a new member of staff in your team who parties until 2am every night including week nights? Do you want to recruit someone who uses inappropriate language on Facebook or appears to bully others? Social media can speak volumes about someone and is often a good way of getting to know people outside of work, so use it to your advantage.

So, you think you have found the ideal new recruit. They have successfully attended two interviews and sailed through their trial with flying colours and you have decided to offer them the job. This can be done informally initially, particularly if you have told them after the trial that you will be in touch before the end of the day with your decision. You may decide to give them a call or drop them an email informing them that they have been successful and this is an ideal time for them to give you feedback. Hopefully they will be pleased and accept the offer but they may have had second thoughts themselves and decide not to accept, or they may, of course, have applied for other, more suitable jobs and accept one of those over yours.

If they do accept the position then it is very important to follow up the email or telephone call with a formal job offer in writing.

I would advise posting out a letter, following the example below, in duplicate and requesting that they sign and return one copy to you to confirm their decision to accept the job. A printable version of this letter is available at www.bloomsbury.com/outstanding-nursery-leader.

Ms A Practitioner
1 Nursery Close
School Lane

20 August 2018

Dear Ms Practitioner

Re: Post of Nursery Practitioner

Further to your interview on 13 August and your subsequent trial today, I am writing to offer you the post of nursery practitioner at Little Acorns Day Nursery.

This offer is subject to:

- Receipt of references, which are, in the subjective opinion of the early years provider, satisfactory.
- Completion of a satisfactory probationary period of six months.
- Completion of the setting's staff suitability self-declaration form and this being satisfactory to the setting.
- A satisfactory enhanced Disclosure and Barring Service (DBS) check with barred lists check, and a subscription to the DBS Update Service.

Your wage will be £9.00 per hour for a full-time position working Monday to Friday, 8am until 6pm, with a 45-minute unpaid lunch and 15-minute unpaid break.

I have attached a copy of the job description and would be grateful if you would confirm acceptance of this offer as outlined above and in the job description, by signing a copy of this letter and returning it to the nursery at your earliest convenience.

May I take this opportunity to welcome you to our nursery and wish you every success in your new post.

Yours sincerely,

A. Manager

Always ascertain when the candidate would like you to apply for references. It is always better for them to hand in their notice before you apply for a reference and therefore a discussion about this is the best way forward. This will also confirm a likely start date for them to join your team.

Probationary periods are dependent on each setting but I personally feel that six months in a nursery is satisfactory. Anything less can be a problem, as it is often difficult to really get to know someone over a short period of time and the new recruit will need time to get to know staff, children and parents, in addition to learning the procedures of the nursery and getting to grips with how things are done in a new setting. I personally think that six months will give you time to ascertain whether the person really fits in and whether they are an asset to the team – if they aren't then in all honesty you don't need them!

It is important to explain what you expect from the new employee. A job description is vital and this should set out exactly what you expect of them in the capacity of the role they are employed to do and inform them of who they are answerable to. You will need to explain the policies and procedures of the nursery and show them what everyday practice looks like in your setting. Remember they may have come from another nursery where things are done very differently and if you have specific ways of doing things this must be made clear.

References

It is essential that you obtain references for all new recruits. Whilst a glowing reference is not a guarantee that the new employee will be infallible, it is a good sign that they have performed well and been a valued member of the team in their last employment. Jobs are usually dependent on a good reference from past employers but there may be times, for whatever reason, that you are unable to get a reference. Perhaps, for example, the setting they previously worked for has closed or their former boss may be particularly vindictive or the company's policy is not to give references.

Employers are not obliged to give a reference but all references must be fair and accurate, and a bad reference, if deemed unfair or misleading by the employee, can be challenged. It is for this reason that many companies only provide 'factual' references, which include the employee's job title, a description of the role they performed, their start and end dates, time off sick and whether there is a live disciplinary on file.

Induction

All new employees should have an induction that formally introduces them to their new job and sets out the important things they need to know, such as fire escapes, health and safety procedures, the use of protective clothing and so forth, and the induction should take into account the policies and procedures of the setting, giving clear instructions of what is expected of the employee. Inductions should not be rushed and should take place over several weeks so that new recruits can fully understand their role and what is expected of them. The forms below provide an example of an induction and give an idea as to how in-depth the induction process is. You will find printable versions of these forms at www.bloomsbury.com/outstanding-nursery-leader.

STAFF INDUCTION			
NAME_____ JOB ROLE_____DATE_____			
INTRODUCTION TO A NURSERY			
First day	**Date completed**	**Employee signature**	**Inductor signature**
Tour around nursery			
Office			
Kitchen			

Toilet			
Pre-school			
Toddlers			
Babies			
Children's washrooms and changing facilities			
Washing and drying facilities			
Storage areas			
Introduction to staff members, children and parents			
Emergency contact details			
Health and safety			
Fire and emergency procedure			
Exits			
Meeting point			
Location of fire extinguishers			
External doors			
Closing of gates between areas To be checked before children allowed out. Gate at front to have catch in place.			
Location of first aid boxes and mobile first aid bags			

Personal protective clothing Disposable gloves and aprons are available in all children's toilets and changing rooms. Aprons and gloves must be worn when dealing with any bodily fluid.			
Food and drink			
Children's food allergies and intolerances List in the kitchen and in all rooms. Cook provides alternative choice.			
Food allergy awareness Food allergy folder contains a list of all ingredients in every dish along with information regarding cross-contamination. A list of allergens is on display in the kitchen, office and every room.			
Staff food If you bring food from home for lunch that needs to be kept cool you may keep it in the allocated fridge in the staff room.			

You may use the microwave to warm your own food in the staff room. Hot food must be kept away from the children and eaten in the allocated area at lunchtime.			
Hot drinks Must not be consumed in areas where children are present.			
Mobile telephones Mobiles are to be kept in the office. If you wish to use your mobile at lunchtime or during breaks you will need to do so outside or in the staff room.			

STAFF INDUCTION			
NAME_____ JOB ROLE_____DATE_____			
First week	**Date completed**	**Employee signature**	**Inductor signature**
The nursery's organisational history and background			
Pay details			
Bank details			
Mission statement			
DBS			

Dress code or uniform			
Holidays Holiday entitlement, request forms			
Sickness The first three days of sickness will not be paid. Days taken after this can be claimed as statutory sick pay on production of a doctor's sick note.			
Absenteeism and lateness			
Discipline and complaints			
Mentor Name			
Training and development All staff are required to take training. The training calendar is displayed on the notice board in the staff room. Training needs will be identified at supervisions.			
First Aid Certificate Renewal date			
Safeguarding Certificate Renewal date			
Food Hygiene Certificate Renewal date			
Key person system Each key person is allocated a small group of children who are to be their key children.			

Child observations Observation undertaken			
Development files After allocation of key children			
Nappy-changing procedure Gloves and apron to be worn. No child to be left unattended.			
Observed nappy change			
Feeding babies Babies must be held when fed and never propped up on their own.			
Bottles Parents bring their own bottles for their children's milk. Bottles to be named.			
Sterilisation			
Cleaning schedules Each room has its own cleaning schedule.			

	Date completed	Employee signature	Inductor signature
Contract of employment			
1st staff observation			
1st supervision meeting			
2nd staff observation			

2nd supervision meeting			
Appraisal			
Evaluation form			

STAFF INDUCTION			
NAME_____ JOB ROLE_____ DATE_____			
Policies (to be signed when read and understood)	**Date completed**	**Employee signature**	**Inductor signature**
Safeguarding children			
Safeguarding children and child protection			
Equality of opportunity			
Supporting children with special educational needs			
Positive behaviour			
Admissions			
Role of key person			
Home visiting			
Transitional			
Health and safety			
Sun protection			
Risk assessment			

Nappy changing			
Recording and reporting of accidents and incidents			
Administering medicines			
Managing children with allergies or who are sick or infectious			
First aid			
Food and drink			
Food hygiene			
Animals in the setting			
No smoking			
Fire safety and evacuation			
Record keeping			
Provider records			
Parental involvement			
Partnership			
Admissions			
Employment			
Student placements			
Whistleblowing			

Probationary periods

Probationary periods are essential. As I mentioned earlier, six months is a good timescale to set for a probationary period. At the end of this period everyone should know whether the arrangement is working, although it often takes much less time than six months to know whether someone is right for the role. Six months gives you time to look at things from all perspectives and, if the employee is part time, it will give them a chance to settle in and learn the nursery's procedures. This is not to say that, if someone is clearly unsuitable, you have to wait six months before ending their employment.

Probationary reviews can, and should, take place during the set probationary period. If you feel the new recruit needs to improve in a specific area, then discuss this with them at a probationary review meeting. Remind the new employee that they are still in their probationary period and explain that you have some concerns about their practice. If the concern is minor then there is every possibility that the employee can improve and therefore successfully pass their probation and become a valued member of your team. However, if you have major concerns, which hopefully you won't if you have carried out interviews and trials as outlined earlier in this chapter, then you need to tackle these issues sooner rather than later. Speak to the new employee and explain your concerns. Ask for their opinions – it could be something they are unaware of and can put right. If you do not feel that the new recruit is as suitable as you had initially hoped, then you have two options: you could extend their probationary period, outlining exactly what improvements need to be made, or you could terminate their contract, explaining exactly why you feel things are not working out.

Terminating contracts is never an easy thing to do. It can be upsetting and is obviously detrimental to the employee's future job prospects. It is also time-consuming, as you will have to start the whole procedure of advertising and interviewing all over again, and of course it causes uncertainty amongst staff, children and parents, as they will have been introduced to the new member of staff. However, none of these factors must deter you from doing the right thing. If you have made a mistake and employed someone who you later feel is unsuitable then you *must* rectify things, however difficult and time-consuming that might be.

Continuing to turn a blind eye to an unsuitable member of staff could lead to years of problems, and no manager can claim to be outstanding if they take the easy way out when sensing a potential problem.

Disciplinary and grievances

Staff problems can happen at any time, in any workplace and with any manager. Problems do not only come about from new recruits who are learning the ropes or may be unsure of the settings policies and procedures. Problems can arise from longstanding staff, those whose employment history has previously been unblemished or those holding senior roles whom you have come to depend on. Whatever the problem, and whomever it concerns, it must be dealt with professionally and in confidence.

It may be that you personally have noticed a problem with a member of staff or it may be that your deputy, supervisor, another member of staff or even a parent has noticed a problem and reported it to you.

When carrying out a disciplinary or dealing with a grievance it is very important that you follow current guidance and legislation. Never jump in with both feet accusing a member of staff of something just because a parent has made a complaint, for example. Situations must be investigated thoroughly and fairly before any decisions are made. The following case studies will introduce some scenarios you may have to deal with as a nursery manager.

Case study 1

Employee A turns up for work five minutes late looking unwell. His uniform is creased and looks unclean and he appears tired and withdrawn.

He immediately goes to the staff room and makes a cup of coffee, giving no explanation as to why he is late. When his supervisor asks him to come into the room as he is required in ratio, he replies, 'I am a bit tired and hungover and I need a coffee to wake me up.'

Your supervisor immediately reports her concerns to you. How would you deal with this situation?

Spend a few minutes thinking about how you would deal with this scenario. Make notes explaining what you would do next and why. Do you see this as a case for instant dismissal? Do you consider this to be cause for a disciplinary? Would you allow the member of staff to have a cup of coffee and then continue working?

There are, of course, a number of things you need to look at here before any major decisions are made but the safety of the children must be paramount in any decisions you do make.

In a situation like this, no matter how you may feel personally about a member of staff allegedly turning up for work under the influence of alcohol, you must remember that, at this stage, it is 'alleged' and nothing is definite or proven.

As the manager you will need to make a number of decisions:

- Is the member of staff fit to be at work?

- Is the member of staff a potential danger to the children?

- Is the member of staff a potential danger to himself or other members of the team?

- Is this the first time something like this has happened concerning this member of staff or is it a regular occurrence?

The situation will need to be investigated thoroughly, and this must be done following the company's disciplinary procedures, before any final decisions are made. A number of outcomes may be possible:

- The member of staff may be disciplined but allowed to remain in work.

- The member of staff may be exonerated.

- The member of staff may be suspended pending investigation.

- The member of staff may be dismissed.

Case study 2

A parent has asked to speak to you in private. You take her to the office, when she discloses that she has just witnessed a member of staff handle a child 'roughly'. She says the child was not her own but that she was concerned that staff were allowed to do this and wanted to know what would be done about it.

How would you respond to this parent?

As the nursery manager, you have an obligation to deal with accusations of this kind. Again, you need to investigate things before making any decisions. Refrain from discussing anything other than the facts. What did the parent actually witness? What was said? Who was involved? Don't allow the parent to involve you in a discussion about the member of staff in general and never make your mind up at this point as to who is at fault. You need to tell the parent that you will investigate her concerns and deal with it appropriately. You must then follow the necessary company procedures of investigation and, if necessary, take the disciplinary route.

It is sometimes easy for managers, particularly those who have worked with members of staff for a long time, to take the side of their colleagues and see parents as causing unnecessary problems, but it is always worth remembering that everyone is human and, as mentioned in Chapter 1, your role of 'counsellor' could uncover a personal problem experienced by a member of staff that is impacting on their work – all these things need to be looked at before any decisions are made. Once again, you are dealing with an 'alleged' situation and 'facts' need to be ascertained before decisions are made.

Separating the wheat from the chaff

Whilst there may be times when you have to deal with a specific incident that has been reported to you, managers also need to challenge more systematic poor practice. If a member of the team is turning out to be ineffective, then they must be challenged. Everyone can have a bad day but it is the members of staff who are constantly negative and resentful who can have a huge impact on the rest of the team. Childcare settings should be happy, lively environments where children have fun and enjoy their time. Employing staff with little or no enthusiasm will soon have a devastating effect, not only on the children but also on the rest of the team. Monitoring staff will soon highlight those whose attitude and work ethic need challenging.

Sick days

As a manager you need to keep abreast of the number of sick days your staff are having. Is there a pattern to staff absences? If so, can this pattern be explained? For example, do certain members of staff have regular sick days on Mondays and Fridays? Is this to enable them to extend their weekends? Are they hungover from partying all weekend and not turning up for work on Monday? Sick days are difficult to manage in the childcare sector as you simply cannot 'put the job off'. Ratios must be maintained at all times and a high level of staff sickness is quite simply unacceptable.

Whilst it is important to remember that some sick days are genuine, it is also your job as the manager to understand which members of staff are regularly absent and deal with them appropriately.

Whistleblowing

Whistleblowing is when a person reports any kind of information or behaviour that is deemed unsafe or unethical within an organisation, and in nursery settings it is essential to safeguard and promote the welfare of children. All settings should have a whistleblowing policy and staff must be trained to know how to identify potential problems and how to report them.

Below is an example of a whistleblowing policy.

SAFEGUARDING CHILDREN:
WHISTLEBLOWING POLICY

Our setting safeguards and promotes the welfare of all children in our care. This whistleblowing policy is in place to support this. All staff are made aware of this policy at the initial staff induction and are clear what behaviour is expected and what is not acceptable.

We aim to create a culture of safe working practice where staff recognise and acknowledge that they are free, able and encouraged to express concerns they may have about childcare practice within our setting.

All staff must acknowledge their individual duty to bring matters of concern to the attention of their senior manager. Although this can be difficult, this is particularly important where the welfare of children may be at risk.

Staff members within the setting may be the first to recognise that some-thing is wrong; however, they may not be able to express concerns out of feeling disloyal to colleagues or out of fear of harassment and victimisa-tion. These feelings, however natural, must never result in a child being put at risk.

Don't think what if I'm wrong – think what if I'm right.

Reasons for whistleblowing:

- Each individual has a responsibility for raising concerns about unacceptable practice or behaviour.
- To prevent problems worsening or widening.
- To protect and reduce risk to others.
- To prevent becoming implicated yourself.

What stops people from whistleblowing?

- Starting a chain of events that will spiral.
- Disrupting work.
- Fear of getting it wrong.
- Fear of repercussions or damaging careers.
- Fear of not being believed.

How to raise a concern:

- You should voice your concerns, suspicions or uneasiness as soon as you feel you can. The earlier the concern is expressed, the easier and sooner action can be taken.
- Try to pinpoint what practice is concerning you and why.
- Give names, dates and places where you can.
- A member of staff is not expected to prove the truth of an allegation but you will need to demonstrate sufficient grounds for concern.
- Approach your immediate manager.
- If you feel that you cannot approach your manager then contact the Local Area Designated Officer (LADO), your Safeguarding Advice Line or Ofsted Whistleblowing on 08456 404046.

What happens next?

- You will be given information on the progress of any enquiries.
- Every step will be taken to ensure you are protected from harassment or victimisation.

- No action will be taken against you if the concerns prove to be unfounded and were raised in good faith.
- Malicious allegations may be considered as a disciplinary offence.

'Absolutely without fail challenge poor practice or performance. If you ignore or collude with poor practice it makes it harder to sound the alarm when things go wrong.'

Sounding the Alarm, Barnardos (1999)

Remuneration

Whether or not you are personally involved in the financial side of things will depend on whether you are working in a private or voluntary-run setting. Privately-run nurseries need to make a profit to be sustainable. However, all organisations must conform to the law with regard to remunerating their staff, which includes paying them the minimum wage and providing a pension scheme. If you are responsible for this side of things then you will need to know the correct, up-to-date information.

Minimum wage

The current law states the following minimum amounts must be paid in wages. Note the rates change every April so check www.gov.uk/national-minimum-wage-rates for annual updates.

Year	25 and over	21 to 24	18 to 20	Under 18	Apprentice
2018	£7.83	£7.38	£5.90	£4.20	£3.70

Source: www.gov.uk/national-minimum-wage-rates

Pensions

Following a change in legislation regarding workplace pensions and the introduction of 'auto enrolment', all employers are now obliged to at least ask all members of staff if they wish to join the workplace pension scheme whilst automatically enrolling others into the scheme.

Legislation

The new legislation stipulates that if employees are aged between 22 and 65 years old and earn in excess of £834 per calendar month, they are an **eligible employee** and therefore **must** be automatically enrolled into the workplace pension scheme. If they do not meet the above criteria, then the employer must give them the option to join the pension scheme. If an employee's total earnings for the month exceed £486 and they choose to opt in, then the employer must also contribute into the pension scheme at the same rate as if they were deemed to be eligible. If the employee's monthly earnings are less than the £486 threshold and they choose to opt in, the employer is not obliged to contribute but must assist in providing them with access to a pension scheme.

Pension contributions

Under the new legislation, both employer and employee have to contribute to the pension scheme. The contribution amounts will increase between 2018 and 2019 as follows:

	Employer	Employee
April 2018 – April 2019	2%	3%
April 2019 onwards	3%	5%

Source: www.gov.uk/workplace-pensions/what-you-your-employer-and-the-government-pay

Both the employer and employee contributions documented above will be subject to qualifying earnings.

Qualifying earnings are defined as earnings between £112 and £826.92 per week or £833 and £3,583 per month (these figures are expected to change annually), and include salary, bonuses, commission, overtime, maternity pay, statutory sick pay plus any other pay element.

Opting out

If an employee decides that they don't want to put money aside for their retirement just yet, they have the right to opt out. They must do this within the opt-out period, which is normally one month from the date the enrolment begins.

Opting out essentially means employees are treated as though they were never enrolled into the pension scheme. If an employee changes their mind after opting out, they can opt back in again if they want to. Employers have a duty to make that happen once in any 12-month period if employees request this. If an employee chooses to opt out they will normally be automatically re-enrolled back into the pension scheme at a later date.

State pension

A company pension scheme has no effect on an employee's state pension entitlement. If an employee is unsure about what their state pension is likely to be or when their state pension will come into force, they should complete a BR19 form and post it to the Department for Work and Pensions (DWP). This form can be found by searching for 'BR19 form' online and the DWP address should be on the form.

Rewarding good staff

Whilst it is important for a manager to know how to recruit new staff for the team, it is equally important that they recognise and reward good staff who are already employed. Good staff retention is important for any business. It provides a solid team and instils customers with confidence. Long-serving members of staff provide families with a familiar face and this is particularly important in the childcare sector, when parents may be bringing their children to the setting over a long period of time, with younger siblings following on from the older child. Stability and familiarity are key for children as well, as they will feel safe and secure when they know the staff.

Rewarding long service need not be expensive; in fact it need not cost anything financially at all. Consider having an award ceremony, for example, and try to include parents and children in order to show the member of staff just how valued they are.

Finding ways of retaining staff can be tricky. The childcare sector is notoriously low paid; therefore by thinking of other ways to recognise and reward good or long-standing practice, managers can make their team members feel valued at work.

Chapter 3
Communication

The ability to communicate effectively is essential for any manager. Communication is the underlying secret of exceptional leaders and there is a knack of communicating effectively. Get it right and you will achieve your goals; get it wrong and you will waste valuable time and effort.

It is probably true to say that, beyond productivity, communication is used to:

- motivate
- inspire
- reassure
- guide.

Day-to-day discussions

Although it is important to have regular set meetings with staff, it is equally important to have *effective* day-to-day conversations. In order to communicate effectively, leaders must understand and consider the needs and level of comprehension of their audience. Being a great orator with the ability to conduct presentations and training is all well and good, providing you are able to do this on a level that is understood by staff of all abilities. Always bear in mind that your team will consist of staff of varying ages with varying experience and qualifications, and you will need to be able to reach out, enthuse and persuade everyone.

When communicating to your team you will need to consider:

- the information you have to share
- the context within which you are communicating
- the method of presentation.

When communicating information to people it is always possible that the message may be misread, and this is increased greatly when communicating in meetings of considerable size, when it may not be possible to ensure that everyone has fully understood what has been said. It is therefore essential that you prepare well for a meeting regardless of how many people are present and what information you need to share. Always:

- Practise what you need to say so that it is clear and systematic.
- Speak the truth – people need to know what you are telling them and asking of them.
- Consider your audience – their age, ability, understanding and experience.
- Avoid using unnecessary jargon – you may know what it means but if staff don't then you may as well be speaking in a different language and you will quickly lose your audience's attention.
- Be confident – know your facts.
- Confirm that your audience has understood what you have said. This can be done by inviting questions.
- Listen.

It is important to remember that communication in the modern day is far from just the simple spoken word. In a world of technology, the spoken word has been taken over by email, Facebook, Twitter, LinkedIn and so on, and these are all ways that your staff may choose to communicate and ways that must be monitored to avoid risk to reputation.

The business should have effective communication policies in place so that staff are under no illusions when it comes to the information they choose to share on social media. Social media is often used to vent anger and frustrations and many people upload images of nights out, which, if seen by customers using your service, may result in loss of revenue and complaints. Staff may see it as being completely harmless and none of the company's business if they are posting antics in their own time, but if they have befriended customers who can view the posts then there are potential problems for you as a manager.

Staff meetings

Not all leaders are born social speakers and being a confident orator takes practice. There is no excuse for a manager to be ill prepared for a meeting, as this will lead to a lack of respect and credibility, which in turn will make for poor leadership. Leaders are never more on show than when they are conducting a meeting and therefore it is essential that you know what you need to say and how you need to say it. The meeting, depending on what it is about, may have the potential to lead to a heated debate, complaints or disagreements, and you will need to keep control of the situation and answer everyone's queries and concerns.

Staff meetings should be undertaken regularly and staff should be given notice of the meetings, preferably with an agenda, several days before the meeting takes place, to allow them to prepare their own questions and responses.

Staff meetings should be structured and planned. Always make sure there are enough seats for everyone attending and ensure that attendees are comfortable and settled before the meeting begins.

The meeting should be opened by reading the agenda, and points on the agenda should be followed in order to avoid overload or other points being raised that are not relevant for discussion. It is essential that the leader commands authority and ensures they are heard but this must never be done through raised voices. Always be pleasant and patient and allow staff to respond without interruption. It is important that you allow everyone to participate whilst managing domination by taking a positive approach. There will always be some staff who are more out-spoken than others but they should not be allowed to monopolise the meeting at the expense of others. A good leader listens to their staff and never is this more important than when in a group meeting. Listening to staff does not just entail noting what they are saying verbally but it also takes into account their body language, eye contact and the way they correspond with one another when you are speaking. Are your staff interested, alert, focused or do they appear bored and unengaged? At the end of the meeting, summarise the points and decisions and ask the minute-taker if they need anything clarifying, before concluding the meeting and thanking everyone for their time. It is important to try to finish the meeting on time.

There are a number of reasons why staff meetings are held. For example, you may have an important message to convey, which needs to be done when everyone is together, you may be looking for new ideas or you may need to incorporate some in-house training. Whatever the reason for the meeting, it is the manager's job to decide whether a team meeting is the most effective way to convey the information in question or whether alternative ways may be more productive. Staff meetings are often seen as necessary but boring additions to the already long day and therefore a manager who can come up with new and interesting ideas will have a better chance of engaging staff and ensuring co-operation. For example, incorporating games and ordering in a takeaway may help to put staff at ease and give them the opportunity to share their own thoughts and ideas. Having a meeting whereby only the manager speaks and there is no input at all from staff is pretty pointless; after all, how do you know if anyone is in agreement with your ideas and suggestions? How do you know that staff will implement them?

Depending on the size of the setting you might like to carry out small-group staff meetings of maybe six to ten people rather than across the whole nursery, which might employ over 30 members of staff. Smaller groups are usually more focused and willing to contribute ideas. It is paramount that the manager listens to and values everyone's suggestions and not just those from senior staff or those who work closely with them. The views of everyone in the setting across the whole workforce are essential in order to achieve outcomes that are effective and reciprocal.

Exercise

Type up an agenda of points to be discussed with staff. Once you have your agenda, decide which points need to be discussed in an informal, small-group meeting and which points need to be addressed in a formal staff meeting. Practice makes perfect and therefore all managers should be prepared for questions and feedback once points on the agenda have been discussed with staff. It pays to be prepared so practise what you will discuss at the meeting beforehand. Rehearse what you need to say and how you will say it and anticipate the responses of staff and how you can reply. Not all managers are good orators and nerves can be an issue when chairing staff meetings, even for the most experienced of managers, as it is not always possible to anticipate the response from members of staff. Being prepared will enable you to reassure staff of any points you are discussing whilst remaining in control of the meeting.

A wise manager will know that, even after a successful meeting, not everyone will be on board with the decisions made, regardless of whether they say they are. It is easy during a meeting for staff to nod their heads in agreement and say they will do what is asked of them but this may not automatically happen in the near future and you, as the manager, will have to guide them going forward. Making decisions is not always easy but leaders need to lead and, armed with the right information, you should be able to make the right decisions. Managers who refuse to take responsibility and let things slide will generate an uncertain team, lacking clarity and guidance, and this is not good for any business. Rest assured wrong decisions will be made – we are, after all, human – but it is best to make a wrong decision with the right intentions than to shun responsibility.

When making decisions leaders need to have a clear view of the desired outcome. You will need to decide whether the decision you are making is routine or urgent and whether it needs to be made immediately or can be thought through and planned in time. Decisions should never be solely the manager's unless they are critical and need to be implemented immediately with no time for consultation. However, it is important to remember that staff can be difficult at times and be demanding if things are not seen to take shape immediately. Emotional responses to problems are rarely good, as they leave us vulnerable and out of control. Quick decisions may backfire and it is therefore always preferable to allow time to think things through before making any important decisions, and you should refuse to be cajoled or bullied.

A good manager will know how to prioritise and understand which decisions are urgent and which are not. In order to do this you need to:

- Think about the problem and what it entails.
- Get advice if this is possible.
- Think through the advantages and disadvantages of any action you are considering.
- Delegate if necessary.
- Prioritise and refuse to be sidetracked.
- Continually check on progress after a decision has been made.
- Set time aside to review the outcome.

Before making any decision, ensure you are well informed to do so. Avoid knee-jerk reactions and, when you have made a decision, stick by it unless it is absolutely obvious that you have made the wrong one. A manager who continually goes backwards and forwards will lose sight of the goal and the respect of their team. Once a decision has been made you will need to delegate, and you need to be sure that the person you trust to implement your decision is equipped to do so. Do they fully understand what is expected of them? You should set deadlines for targets so that everyone is aware of when and why outcomes will be reviewed.

Supervisions

Ofsted no longer require nursery settings to carry out staff appraisals as these have been replaced by supervisions. In a nutshell, supervisions are more detailed and in depth and allow managers to get a better understanding of their team, discover their assets and find their weaknesses.

It is an Ofsted requirement that all settings have appropriate arrangements in place for the effective supervision of staff.

3.21 Providers must put appropriate arrangements in place for the supervision of staff who have contact with children and families.

Effective supervision provides support, coaching and training for the practitioner and promotes the interests of children. Supervision should foster a culture of mutual support, teamwork and continuous improvement, which encourages the confidential discussion of sensitive issues.

Statutory Framework for the Early Years Foundation Stage
(Department for Education, 2017)

It is important that staff understand what supervisions are and why they are carried out. They are not a means to 'catch them out', but are designed to support staff and identify any issues or potential problems and address them.

3.22 Supervision should provide opportunities for staff to:

- discuss any issues – particularly concerning children's development or wellbeing, including child protection concerns
- identify solutions to address issues as they arise
- receive coaching to improve their personal effectiveness

Statutory Framework for the Early Years Foundation Stage
(Department for Education, 2017)

Supervisions are a necessary requirement and they need to be carried out regularly in order to be effective. So what exactly is a supervision and what does it involve?

Supervisions are a 'safe' time to raise and explore issues of concern and effective (inclusive) practice. They are used to continually improve the quality and safety of each child's experience in the setting.

Supervisions are used to discuss:

- qualifications
- training
- support
- skills

along with ensuring that all staff are aware of the development of their key children and are confident carrying out observations and tracking.

Supervisions provide opportunities to:

- Discuss any issues – particularly those concerning children's development or wellbeing.
- Identify solutions to address issues as they arise.
- Receive coaching to improve their personal effectiveness.

Ofsted inspectors will ask for evidence to evaluate the effectiveness of staff supervision and the impact of these on the wellbeing of children, their learning and development.

It is vital that everyone in the setting has a shared understanding of the purpose of supervisions. Supervisions must:

- Be valued through adequate time.
- Be respectful and professional.
- Be a two-way discussion.
- Allow for action to be agreed and acted on.

Preparing for supervisions

As mentioned above, supervisions are a two-way conversation and we need to steer away from the supervisor asking questions and the supervisee providing all the answers. For the experience to be successful, everyone must play their part.

It is important that staff can prepare for supervisions for them to be effective. You can suggest they consider areas such as:

- Thinking about the times, roles and activities during which they feel most confident and competent, as well as those that make them feel less confident.
- Exceptions – things that have worked particularly well or have resulted in an unforeseen problem.
- New initiatives – things that they think may need changing, such as routines. They may have some suggestions, opinions or ideas that can be backed up by success or difficulty, which need to be discussed.
- Training – they may be able to identify roles, activities and skills that they would like to learn more about to develop their expertise.

One of the main things that will be discussed during the supervision process is the practitioner's key children. Therefore the practitioner will also need to bring their key children's files or records to the meeting and be able to discuss all areas of development of their key children and identify any concerns when asked. This is something that inspectors will do during Ofsted visits.

The following is an example of a staff supervision template that could be used in a nursery setting, with prompts for the manager carrying out the supervision shown in italics. Relevant sections of the Statutory Framework for the Early Years Foundation Stage (Department for Education, 2017) are referred to throughout. A printable version of this form is available at www.bloomsbury.com/outstanding-nursery-leader.

STAFF SUPERVISION

(Staff supervision is a statutory requirement for the Early Years Foundation Stage, 3 April 2017. Sections 3.21 and 3.22, page 21.)

Record of meeting *[The record of the meeting does not need to be written out verbatim.]*

Name of employee: ………………………………………

Role and level of qualification: ………………………………………

Name and position of person leading the meeting: ………………………………

Date: ………………………………………

Time started: ………………………………………

Time finished: ………………………………………

DBS check: *[Include the unique reference number.]* ………………………………

Date obtained: ………………………………………

Any relevant cautions or convictions? *[State the impact, if any, on their current role or responsibilities. A further risk assessment may be required.]*
………………………………………………………………………………
………………………………………………………………………………

Who do you live with and/or any disqualifications through association(s)? *[Refer to sections 3.14–3.18, pages 19 and 20 and also 3.77, page 34.]*
………………………………………………………………………………
………………………………………………………………………………

Discussion about your role and responsibilities (job description/ specification):

....

....

Are you happy in your work?

....

....

What inspires you most?

....

....

What do you find difficult and/or what would you like to change?

....

....

Do you have any concerns or unresolved issues about team members or anything that could adversely affect the smooth running of the nursery?

....

....

Is there any change to your health that may affect your performance at work? *[Refer to section 3.19, page 20 and 3.64, page 31; a health care plan may be required.]*

....

....

If applicable, any progress on actions raised at the previous meeting:

....

....

Who are your key children and what are their ages in months? *[Consider bonding and attachment.]*

....

....

View and discuss key children's development files and how well they are maintained. Include assessments, observations, planning, home learning/ partnership with parents and any evaluations (focused activities – what went well and what could be done differently?)

....

....

Additional information/extra considerations about key children. For example, EAL; SEND; child attends another EYFS setting; looked after child; progress check at age 2 etc. *[Refer to child's development file.]*

....

....

Do you have any concerns about the children's welfare or learning and development? Summarise any advice given to improve children's welfare and to enhance your personal effectiveness.

....

....

As a reflective practitioner, how and when do you evaluate your activities with the children and plan next steps? *[Evaluations are best completed after a 'focused' activity with the practitioner's key children. Next steps are usually planned when the children's assessments have been updated and following written observations, which help to identify any gaps in children's achievements (development bands). The information obtained is then used to inform weekly activity plans for the group, which are usually displayed for parents to view. Staff should be able to explain how these activities can be adapted and extended to meet the individual needs of children (differentiation). The information obtained is also used to inform individualised planning recorded on the children's next steps in partnership with parents to promote home learning. This is a good opportunity to check 'Notes' in children's assessments to make sure parents have countersigned and dated next steps.]*

....

....

Do you have any child protection concerns regarding your key children or any child who attends the nursery? *[Refer to section 3, page 16.]*

....

....

How do we safeguard children at the nursery? *[How do we keep children safe? The following are some of the many responses staff could give: maintain medication, accident, incident and pre-existing injury forms in partnership with parents; maintain a daily register (time of arrival and departure and child's key person); complete risk assessments before trips and outings; keep doors closed/locked and make sure child safety gates are closed; maintain appropriate adult:child ratios (1:3 baby room; 1:4 toddler room and 1:8 pre-school room); supervise children's indoor and outdoor play at all times; check sleeping children regularly; assist children in the bathroom; potty/ toilet training and hand washing; support small groups of children at snack* *and meal time and make sure they receive the help they may need to cut solid food into small pieces to minimise the risk of choking; maintain a paediatric first aid certificate; operate a password system (departures); make sure children's emergency contact details are kept up to date; obtain parents' written consent to get medical assistance in an emergency; make sure bottle-fed children are held and routinely winded; make sure staff are deployed in specific areas and to specific activities to keep children safe.]*

....

....

Have you practised the emergency evacuation procedure? If so, when? Any comments/concerns?

....

....

Discuss the main aim and objectives of the nursery's child protection policy and procedure: *[The welfare of children is paramount. All adults have a duty of care to protect children from abuse and neglect. All adults working at the nursery have a responsibility to implement the three Rs: recognise signs of abuse and neglect, and record and report them to the nursery manager and registered provider.]*

....

....

In relation to child protection (CP), who are the lead practitioners at the nursery and how accessible should they be? *[The nursery manager and designated and trained child protection/safeguarding officers. They should be contactable at all times during opening hours.]*

....

....

Who must they inform if there is a CP concern (referral) and what is the timescale for notifications? *[Ofsted should be contacted as soon as is reasonably practicable, but always within 14 days (refer to sections 3.77 and 3.78, pages 34–5). The local safeguarding children's board (LSCB – local authority/social services) should also be notified as soon as is reasonably practicable.]*

....

....

How often should the lead practitioner(s) attend child protection training courses? *[The designated child protection/safeguarding officer should update* *knowledge and understanding on safeguarding every two years and complete a refresher course annually.]*

....

....

What are the signs and/or symptoms of abuse and neglect? *[The following gives an indication of some of the many responses staff could give:* **Neglect***: exceptionally poor personal care/hygiene; soiled and/or poor fitting clothing; inappropriately dressed according to the weather; repeatedly soiled nappies at the beginning of each session and no available change of clothing; attention-seeking behaviour, hunger, thirst or failure to thrive.* **Emotional abuse***: unusual hyperactivity or shyness; withdrawn and/or anger issues.* **Physical abuse***: unexplained, unlikely or inconsistent accounts of bruising or burns; black eyes; broken limbs; soreness and/or stiffness; difficulty moving.* **Sexual abuse***: soreness and/or stiffness; difficulty moving; secrecy; reluctant to undress and/or use the potty and/or toilet; bleeding and/or bruising around the rectum, vagina and mouth; sexually transmitted infections.]*

....

....

What is the procedure to follow if an allegation of abuse is made against a member of staff? *[The nursery manager/registered provider will notify Ofsted and the LCSB or local authority designated officer. The nursery manager/registered provider will suspend the member of staff until a full investigation has been completed.]*

....

....

How do we promote e-safety within the setting and in partnership with parents? (Where applicable include out of school club.) *[E-safety is an extension to CP/safeguarding procedures. E-safety includes procedures for the safe use of cameras and images, mobile phones and the internet. Parental controls should be used on ICT resources, such as the home computer and tablets. DVDs should be age-appropriate; staff should think about the age rating of films, including videos on YouTube. A 'Universal' rating is suitable for children in early years settings.]*

....

....

What are the arrangements that cover the safe use of mobile phones and cameras within the nursery? *[Staff should turn their mobile phones off when*

*they come on duty and they should be stored securely in the office. They
can be used at break time and home time. With the manager's permission,
they can be used to make urgent calls. The nursery provides a camera to
take photographs of children's achievements, which are usually maintained
in children's development files and linked to specific areas of learning and
development bands to show parents how children are progressing towards the
early learning goals. Photographs are also used on wall displays and, with
parents' written consent, in newsletters and other media to promote the work
of the nursery.]*

....
....

**The internet is now regarded as an essential resource to support teaching
and learning. How do we use it at the nursery and what safeguards are
in place to promote children's safety and welfare?** *[The following gives
an indication of some of the many responses staff could give: ensure the
nursery's computer and laptop are fitted with a recommended firewall;
ensure computers and laptops are fitted with recommended anti-virus software; provide the children with shortcuts to favourite sites; visit all the
sites first so that you are aware of the content and are able to support
and extend children's learning; be aware that all image searches on search
engines can be risky; search for images on sites used in education, e.g.
Microsoft Gallery; position the computer so that it faces out into the room,
enabling you to monitor internet use easily; provide rules for sharing so
that children can collaborate, e.g. have two chairs at the computer, ensuring
you provide an active role for the child in the 'waiting seat' by calling it the
'helping seat' and teach children how to turn-take using a sand timer for
each child's turn.]*

....
....

**What safeguards are in place when staff use the office PC and/or the nursery's
laptop?** *[Staff should have regard for the Data Protection Act (DPA) 1998 and
the Freedom of Information Act 2000, which is a statutory requirement (section
3.69, page 32). The nursery should also have regard for the General Data
Protection Regulation (GDPR) 2018. The nursery must also be registered
with the Information Commissioner's Office (section 3.70, page 32). The
nursery acts as a holder, known as a custodian or data controller, of personal
information. The nursery recognises its moral duty to make sure that data is
handled properly and confidentially at all times, whether it is held on paper*

or electronically. This covers the whole lifecycle, including: obtaining personal data, storing and securing personal data, using personal data and disposing of or destroying personal data. Important data and documents should be routinely and securely 'backed up'.]

....

....

What safeguards are in place when using email? *[Maintaining the security of a mail system is an ongoing process, requiring constant effort, resources and vigilance. It is important to protect against malware with malware scanning and spam filtering capabilities. The nursery should conduct awareness and training activities for users, so they can recognise malicious mail messages and attachments and know how to handle and report them appropriately.]*

....

....

What safeguards are in place for online communication and social networking? *[Social networking for personal use is not allowed at work. Staff should have regard for The Employee Handbook, which includes guidelines for social networking, including parents.]*

....

....

What is your understanding of fundamental British values in early years? *[The fundamental British values of democracy, rule of law, individual liberty, mutual respect and tolerance for those with different faiths and beliefs are already implicitly embedded in the Early Years Foundation Stage. For example, staff promote personal, social and emotional development (PSEd) and understanding the world (people and communities).]*

....

....

What is your understanding of Prevent duty in early years and working in partnership with parents? *[The Counter-Terrorism and Security Act 2015 places a duty on early years providers 'to have due regard to the need to prevent people from being drawn into terrorism'. The Prevent duty is in place to ensure fundamental British values are not compromised. The three Rs are important here again – staff must recognise, record and report the following: people or institutions that actively promote intolerance of other faiths, cultures and races; people or institutions who fail to challenge gender stereotypes and the*

*routine segregation of girls and boys; people or institutions who actively iso-
late children from their wider community. Patterns of absence and prolonged
absence may be indicators of safeguarding issues. Therefore, the nursery
should have systems in place to manage and monitor unusual and unexpected
absences. There is no single way of identifying an individual who is likely
to be susceptible to a terrorist ideology. Staff should be alert to changes
in children's and parents' behaviour, which could indicate interventions are
required. Children at risk of radicalisation may display different signs or try
to hide their views.]*

....

....

**What safeguards are in place for children with special educational needs and
disabilities (SEND)?** *[Additional barriers can exist when recognising abuse
and neglect in children with SEND. Therefore, these children face additional
safeguarding challenges. Consider children's personal safety and working in
partnership with parents and others. A consistent and collaborated approach
to CP and safeguarding is required through established risk assessment
processes – for example, multi-disciplinary (multi-agency) care plans agreed
with parents to promote health and personal care, such as potty or toilet
training.]*

....

....

**What safeguards are in place to prevent and report concerns about Female
Genital Mutilation (FGM)?** *[Staff should have regard for the document
issued in April 2016 by HM Government: 'Multi-agency Statutory Guidance
on Female Genital Mutilation'.]*

....

....

What safeguards are in place to review any concern about staff behaviour?
*[The following gives an indication of some of the many responses staff could
give: The Employee Handbook includes various policies that set standards
on how staff should work in the nursery – for example, around the safe use
of mobile phones and cameras and reporting an absence from work; staff
supervision is a statutory requirement and it is an opportunity for the nursery manager to assess and promote staff's knowledge and understanding
of specific policies and procedures, in particular, the Child Protection/*

Safeguarding policy and procedures; supervision is also used to manage underperformance and can support staff by highlighting and focusing on areas that require development.]

....
....

What safeguards are in place to prevent peer-on-peer abuse? *[The following gives an indication of some of the many responses staff could give: the CP policy includes a section on peer-on-peer abuse – for example, children who bully or bite others; incidents will be recorded and countersigned by parents; staff should be mindful of the need for confidentiality; the perpetrator will not be identified but staff must reassure the victim's parents that measures are in place to address the issue.]*

....
....

Should the need arise, how should parents implement the complaints policy and procedure? *[Managing complaints and working in partnership with parents is a statutory requirement (sections 3.74 and 3.75, page 33). Parents are advised to discuss concerns with their child's key person. Parents should notify the room leader if the concern is not addressed according to their wishes. The room leader will notify the nursery manager. The nursery manager will notify the registered provider, who must notify Ofsted of formal complaints. A written record of all complaints and their outcome must be maintained and available for Ofsted to view.]*

....
....

What should we do if the complaint cannot be resolved within the nursery? Include notifications and timescales. *[A copy of the nursery's complaints policy and procedure should be available for parents to view. The registered provider has 28 days to investigate the complaint and will respond in writing to parents. If parents are not satisfied with the outcome they can notify Ofsted. Depending on the nature of the complaint, Ofsted may decide to conduct an unannounced inspection. A copy of the inspection report must be made available to parents and carers of children attending on a regular basis (section 3.75, page 33).]*

....
....

Have you any health and/or safety concerns?

....

....

Feedback from staff/peer observations: suggestions for improvement to enhance the quality of teaching and learning: *[Refer to staff observations and answers given by the employee during this interview.]*

....

....

What further training is required and what training are you interested in attending? *[Consider mandatory staff training, such as paediatric first aid, CP/safeguarding.]*

....

....

Personal professional development following your last 1-2-1 (supervision): *[Include any coursework to complete and the timescale to submit it, courses attended, qualifications gained, etc.]*

....

....

Number of days of annual leave outstanding: ......

Authorised annual leave (dates): ....

Employee comments:

....

....

Employee's signature and date: ....

Manager's signature and date: ....

Director's signature and date: ....

Training

Supervisions are useful tools for identifying the training needs of staff. Staff who have been unable to or are unsure how to answer the questions you ask them during supervision may require further training and this is a good time to discuss their training needs with them.

Few local authorities offer free training anymore due to government spending cuts, and the costs can be off-putting for nursery owners on a tight budget. It is therefore essential that the manager identifies who needs training over those who just enjoy attending training courses.

Training should be regularly updated, and the manager needs to know how often training should be updated and have a list of the dates staff have attended training courses so that they can be sure that training hasn't lapsed. First aid, for example, needs to be renewed every three years and safeguarding every two years with annual refreshers.

Training courses are universally offered and can be undertaken in a variety of ways such as in-house or online, but it is essential to concentrate on the compulsory courses and make sure that all staff are up to date with these before looking at doing some of the other courses available.

Staff records

Providers must hold up-to-date staff records for all people living or employed on the premises (Statutory Framework for the Early Years Foundation Stage, section 3.76, page 33; Department for Education, 2017).

The following records should be kept on an employee's personnel file:

1. job application and CV
2. job offer
3. contract
4. references
5. DBS number
6. job description
7. staff details, including home address, telephone number and email address
8. induction
9. health care plan (if applicable – see page 59)
10. holiday details
11. training log
12. certificates
13. supervisions.

Exercise

Spend some time going through the files of your current staff, ensuring that all the above information is included in each. If you don't currently have a training log then start one and ensure that all staff files are regularly updated.

Staff wellbeing

Looking after your staff team is vital for the continued success of the setting. A high staff turnover will bring about uncertainty, and parents may become concerned if staff come and go frequently, as this also makes it difficult for children to bond. For a team to work effectively, staff need to get to know one another well; they need to know each other's strengths and weaknesses so they can support each other on a daily basis. The manager has the added pressure of having to know *all* the staff well rather than just those in their immediate surroundings.

Boosting self-esteem and confidence is important for staff wellbeing. Everyone feels motivated if they feel appreciated and a good manager will recognise and praise achievement on a regular basis. Praising staff can be done in a number of ways, for example:

- A bonus scheme might be introduced – this doesn't have to be a financial reward; it could be an extra day's holiday, for example.
- A noticeboard might display comments showing appreciation.
- You could introduce an employee of the week scheme.

One of the easiest ways to boost staff wellbeing and confidence is to show your team that you trust and value them as individuals. The manager who believes that their team cannot operate without them breathing down their necks will not secure a confident workforce. Staff need to feel they 'belong' in the team and there are many small ways of achieving this, such as organising social events or bringing in cakes to celebrate staff birthdays.

Exercise

Think about ways you can boost the self-esteem of your staff team. Discuss your ideas with your deputy manager or supervisors to ensure that the needs and preferences of all staff are taken into consideration.

You will likely already be aware of Maslow's Hierarchy of Needs (1943), as this is often referred to for the basic needs of children. For example, we know that a child cannot concentrate if their basic needs are not met – if they are tired, hungry or upset. The same principle works for adults and we should be looking at whether the needs of staff, as well as the children, are being met.

Basic needs

- Are staff allowed regular breaks to rejuvenate themselves, especially if they are working in a particularly busy room or with challenging children?

- Is the environment comfortable? Is it warm enough in winter and cool enough in summer?

- Are staff able to access water regularly in order to keep hydrated like the children?

- Is the uniform comfortable? It may look good, but is it practical?

Safety needs

It must be said that most settings are confident with the health and safety regimes they have in place to protect children, but often this gets overlooked when it comes to staff. For example, does your setting have policies in place to protect staff who are:

- pregnant
- working on computers
- sitting or standing for long periods of time
- lifting and handling children?

Social needs

Team-building sessions are useful to help staff to 'bond' and they can provide good opportunities, outside of the workplace, for staff to socialise and get to know each other on another level.

Achievement needs

Managers can support achievement needs through continuing professional development (CPD). Staff supervisions are an ideal opportunity to discuss staff's CPD and to talk about progression.

The good manager will recognise and respect the broad array of strengths and styles that each individual will bring to the team. The larger the team, the more input and ideas will be available. Effective staff teams will include a selection of ideas and styles, which, when amalgamated, produce a secure and productive working base.

Meredith Belbin, a management consultant born in 1926, produced a theory that reflected the importance of respecting and using the varying styles and strengths of every team member. Belbin identified that a team performs well if each team member has clear responsibilities, and he identified nine key roles within his theory:

- **Implementers**: These are the team members who can be relied upon the most to carry out their duties efficiently and effectively. They have a lot of common sense and are dependable and loyal. Their weaknesses include being inflexible and slow to respond to new ideas.

- **Team workers**: These are team members who are good at listening, motivating and supporting others. They are flexible and have a calming influence on other members of staff. Their weaknesses include being indecisive and they will avoid confrontation.

- **Co-ordinators**: These are staff members who show confidence. They are calm and good at encouraging staff to work together to achieve the desired result. They have excellent delegation skills and are quick to identify talent. They can sometimes be seen as manipulative and may delegate their own share of work.

- **Plants**: These are the inventive and creative team members who are good at problem-solving. Their weakness is communication.

- **Specialists:** These are the members of staff who are highly skilled in a subject area – for example, in a nursery setting they might have the role of SENCO. They are inclined to contribute only in certain areas and can dwell on technicalities.

- **Completer-finishers:** Experts in doing tasks well and meeting deadlines, they are inclined to worry and are poor at delegating.

- **Resource investigators:** They are expert communicators and are outgoing and enthusiastic. They tend to run out of steam and lose interest once their initial enthusiasm has passed.

- **Shapers:** These are challenging, dynamic individuals who thrive on pressure but they can be insensitive.

- **Monitors or evaluators:** They are open to all options and are good at judging accurately. They can lack drive and are poor at inspiring others. They may be overcritical at times.

Exercise

Make a list of your own staff team and note next to each which of the above roles you consider each member of staff to fall into. Next analyse how many members of staff fall into each role. Does your team reflect an overall balance or is the scale tipped towards any particular role or roles? Do you consider this to be a problem and, if so, what can you do about it?

Health care plan

In some cases you may need to complete a health care plan for a member of staff. Health care plans are not used just for permanent health problems and it is good practice to introduce one for any member of staff who may be experiencing a health problem, however temporary, to be sure that any necessary adjustments can be introduced to reduce any further problems. Staff on a health care plan need to be regularly monitored and the plan updated.

Below is an example of a health care plan. A printable version of this form is available at www.bloomsbury.com/outstanding-nursery-leader.

HEALTH CARE PLAN

FOR PHYSICAL, MEDICAL AND COMPLEX NEEDS FOR ADULTS IN THE WORKPLACE

Name...	
Date of birth..	Photo
Address.. ....Postcode........................	
Place of work	
Medical diagnosis or condition	

Emergency contacts

In emergencies the first call should be to 999.

Family contacts

Name...

Tel work..................... home..................... mobile..................

Name...

Tel work..................... home..................... mobile..................

Alternative emergency contact

Relationship................................. Name.................................

Tel work..................... home..................... mobile..................

General practitioner/doctor ,,

Telephone number..

Midwife...

Telephone number..

Any other medical practitioner involved (provide contact details)

....

Describe any medical needs and symptoms.

....

Describe your daily care requirements (e.g. meal times, equipment and medication).

....

Describe what constitutes an emergency for yourself and what action to take if this occurs.

....

Do you have any religious or cultural beliefs that may affect any medical treatment?

....

What medication should be administered to yourself in an emergency?

....

It is the responsibility of the staff member to update the setting with medical information and provide medication that is within its expiry date.

....

Where are the required medication and/or medical supplies stored?

....

Person responsible to initiate health care plan review

....

Health care plan review date...

(NO MORE THAN 6 MONTHS FROM DATE OF SIGNATURE)

Are there any additional plans in place?

....

Copies of the health care plan are held by:

....

Designated named person/s trained and agreeing to administer medication:

Name..

Name..

Name..

Name..

I consent to staff administering the above procedure to me.

Signed..Date................

Manager..Date ....

GP/Other medic..Date ....

NOTES

A health care plan should detail all aspects of the member of staff's condition, as well as the medicines and support they need. It should be written in liaison with the health care professionals involved and kept in a place accessible to staff at the nursery and where it can be found quickly should an emergency arise. Training should be arranged for all areas of need, and the health care plan updated regularly.

Chapter 4
Safeguarding and welfare

The 'Working Together to Safeguard Children' document (www.gov.uk/government/publications/working-together-to-safeguard-children--2) was produced by the government in 2015 to provide guidance to help professionals to understand what they need to do, and what they can expect of one another, to safeguard children. The guidance focuses on legal requirements and sets out what both individuals and organisations must do in order to keep children safe. The guidance states that:

> 'Effective safeguarding arrangements in every local area should be underpinned by two key principles:
>
> - safeguarding is everyone's responsibility: for services to be effective each professional and organisation should play their full part; and
> - a child-centred approach: for services to be effective they should be based on a clear understanding of the needs and views of children.'

To fully understand these two key principles, we need to break each down and look at what they mean.

1. **Safeguarding is everyone's responsibility**: It is important that we remember that no single person can have a complete picture of a child's needs and circumstances and it is therefore paramount that children and families receive the right help at the right time in order that concerns are identified promptly and information is shared correctly. A manager needs to understand their own

role and the role of other professionals so that they are confident knowing when and how a referral is made.

2. **A child-centred approach**: It has to be said that failings in safeguarding systems often happen when the needs of the adults are placed ahead of the needs of the children and it is therefore essential that professionals never lose sight of the needs and views of the children they work with. Children must be respected and have stable, trusting relationships with the adults around them in order for their voices to be heard. A child-centred approach is supported by three main pieces of legislation, namely:

- The Children Act 1989
- The Equality Act 2010
- The United Nations Convention on the Rights of the Child (UNCRC)

The Statutory Framework for the Early Years Foundation Stage (Department for Education, 2017) sets out the standards for learning, development and care for children from birth to five years, and section 3 of this document refers solely to safeguarding and welfare requirements, including child protection, staff suitability and training.

Effective safeguarding in a nursery setting requires all staff to be aware of the signs, symptoms and indicators of child abuse and knowing how to report suspected cases. As a nursery manager, it is essential that you are secure in this knowledge and can train your staff accordingly. Safeguarding also involves being compliant with government policy relating to Prevent duty, British values and female genital mutilation (FGM), as well as having clear procedures in terms of e-safety and appropriate staff behaviour.

Signs, symptoms and indicators of child abuse

Whilst the NSPCC report in their latest publication 'How Safe Are Our Children' (www.nspcc.org.uk/globalassets/documents/research-reports/how-safe-children-2017-report.pdf) a downward trend in five-year average death rates for assault, neglect and undetermined intent in England, Northern Ireland and Scotland since 1981, Wales have remained at a similar level to that shown in 1985 and the five-year average death rate in 2015 was 8.5 per million.

The report makes for interesting reading regarding child homicides that were recorded by the police, and which include murder, manslaughter and infanticide. The report shows that out of 61 homicides across the UK in 2015/16, 56 of these occurred in England, with the remaining five being in Scotland. There were no homicides in Wales or Northern Ireland during the same period and the five-year average rate of homicides has declined in the UK over the past decade.

The report also shows that public awareness of the prevalence of abuse and neglect has consistently remained fairly high since 2013, with 61 per cent of people describing abuse and neglect as being 'common'. The report also shows that, since 2013, there has been a nine per cent increase in the proportion of people believing that child abuse and neglect can be prevented and that early intervention to support those who may be struggling has grown in popularity.

The same report indicates an increase in the last five years in recorded offences of cruelty and neglect of children under the age of 16 in England, Wales and Northern Ireland and carried out by a parent or carer. The report associates this increase with the changes to recording practices and the likelihood of abuse being more widely reported. Whilst England, Wales and Northern Ireland's trend has increased, Scotland's was shown to be on the decline in 2015/16, with the lowest volume and rate of recorded cruelty and neglect offences in more than a decade.

In this context, it is absolutely crucial that you and all your staff are aware of child abuse and that you consider your own role in protecting children.

What is abuse?

There is no set pattern for child abuse and it can happen to any child living within any family set-up. Abuse is *usually* carried out by someone that the child knows and trusts – for example, family members and friends – and may, in some circumstances, be committed by those in roles of authority, such as teachers and early years professionals. Abuse is the maltreatment of a child. Abuse can be inflicted by someone causing harm to a child or by someone failing to act to prevent harm from being inflicted. Abuse can be inflicted by adults or children.

When considering whether a child has been abused we should never look solely at their family background and set-up and assume those living in less privileged families are more likely to suffer abuse than those from affluent families whose parents appear to be happily married and successful.

Adults may begin to abuse a child for a number of reasons, including:

- having suffered from abuse themselves
- a lack of parenting skills
- little or no understanding of how to respond to and protect the child
- stress
- separation of child and parent.

The above list is not exhaustive but it outlines some of the reasons why adults may abuse children.

There are six main types of abuse:

- physical abuse
- sexual abuse
- emotional abuse
- neglect
- child sexual exploitation
- online abuse.

Let's consider each of these in turn.

Physical abuse

Physical abuse is either where an injury to a child is done intentionally or when an adult fails to protect a child from being injured or harmed Physical abuse can include many forms, such as:

- The child being hit either using the hand or an implement such as a belt.

- The child being shaken.
- The child being burnt or scalded; this can be done by hot water, an iron, cigarettes, and so forth.
- The child being bitten.
- The child being force-fed.
- The child being allowed access to drugs and alcohol.

Whilst we must be aware that all children will, from time to time, suffer some accidental injuries and most will, at some point, encounter bruises, cuts and even broken bones, we must also be vigilant towards abuse and act on any suspicions immediately. Remember, in cases of suspected abuse it is the child who should be at the centre of any decisions that are made and we must never ignore our suspicions for fear of being wrong.

By understanding how accidental injuries can occur and being able to compare these with suspected abuse, we can build up a clear picture that should help us to determine whether we are dealing with an accident or with abuse.

The main factors to consider are the location and frequency of the injury. Accidental injuries will occur occasionally unless the child is particularly accident-prone and this will become obvious to the staff caring for them, whereas abuse will occur regularly and the child may suffer continually from injuries.

Accidental bruising, cuts and grazes will usually be located in the following areas:

- forehead
- chin
- nose
- knees
- elbows
- forearms
- spine
- hips
- shin.

Non-accidental injuries are more likely to be located in areas that are covered by clothing, such as:

- chest
- stomach
- buttocks
- back of legs
- upper and inner arms
- genital areas
- rectal areas
- soles of the feet
- neck.

Other non-accidental locations of injuries include the lips and mouth, eyes, ears, cheeks and skull, and injuries to these areas can indicate abuse. It is important to look at all the factors when considering whether an injury has been sustained accidentally or intentionally. It is very rare, for instance, for a child to sustain an injury to the mouth unless they have banged themselves. Therefore, if a baby is suffering from a torn frenulum (attachment of the tongue), then this may indicate that they have been force-fed. Suspicions should also be aroused if a child has two black eyes, and the explanations of these types of injuries should be viewed with caution.

Although prolonged patterns of bruising should not automatically be looked at suspiciously, it is important to note down any injuries and look for patterns that may point to the child being abused.

Some children will suffer from bruises, cuts and grazes more often than others and this may simply be because some children are more boisterous and enjoy physical play more than others. However, a child who appears to have varying injuries, which have been borne over a period of time, should be monitored carefully, particularly if they have bruising that appears to have been inflicted over a number of weeks; you will know this by the variation in colours of the bruising. This may indicate that the child is being abused and that injuries are being inflicted regularly. Always treat injury with suspicion if the parent cannot offer a suitable explanation of what has happened and if the child's account of the accident varies considerably to that of the parent. If a child comes to your setting with *any* injury it is vital that you get the parent to complete an 'accident at home' form or a 'pre-existing injury' form, which will request an account of the accident, how the injury was sustained, when and where it happened and a detailed description of the injury, including location, size and colour. This record should be kept along with a chronological record for each child. Through monitoring these records, and discussions with staff, the manager should be able to see whether any patterns arise that show frequent, unexplained or suspicious injuries.

Bruising

Bruising is the most common physical injury a child is likely to suffer and most children will have their fair share of bruising over the years when they are beginning to crawl, walk and become more mobile. It is important to bear in mind that mobility is strongly related to bruising, so a young baby who is not yet mobile is unlikely to suffer from bruising, and any child who is not crawling or walking but who sustains injuries of this nature should be viewed with suspicion.

Not all bruises are suspicious, however, and it is important to know what to look for when considering whether a child is being abused. Bruises that have been inflicted through abuse are often located on areas of the body where the flesh is soft, such as the buttocks, abdomen and cheeks. Groups or clusters of bruising may indicate that a child has been grabbed and these will be more apparent on the upper arms or on the thighs. Bruising sustained in areas such as the face, ears, hips, backs of legs, hands or feet may indicate that a child has tried to protect themselves, and any injuries that show an 'imprint' may suggest that either a hand or an object has been used to inflict an injury, such as the buckle of a belt.

All practitioners in a day care setting should be suitably trained in safeguarding and it is recommended that both online and, if possible, in-house training is carried out regularly to ensure practitioners are up to date with regulations regarding child abuse and are confident about knowing how to recognise and report any suspicions.

Exercise

Despite the fact that all practitioners working in a childcare setting should be suitably trained in safeguarding procedures, it is probably true to say that, unless these procedures are being used regularly, it is easy to forget what has been taught. Think about how you, as a manager, can ensure that your staff do not forget these important procedures and make a list of ways to regularly 'test' staff on their knowledge, for example through in-house training and bringing the procedures to staff meetings.

It is probably true to say that physical abuse is the easiest form of abuse to recognise, quite simply because the injuries are visible. However, in order to ascertain whether the injuries are the result of an accident or, in fact, abuse, we need to look for other signs and be available should the child wish to talk. If the child is old enough to tell you what has happened then ask them. Always allow the child to tell you in 'their own words' and never ask leading questions. Use open questions rather than closed questions and give the child the time they need to explain things. Usually children who have sustained an injury accidently will be quite open and honest and offer an explanation without any difficulty – sometimes they may even be proud of how brave they have been and love telling the story! However, if a child appears nervous or anxious then this may be a sign that they have been intentionally harmed and your suspicions may be aroused. A child who is being physically abused may, in addition to having physical injuries, also show signs such as:

- confusion
- fear
- shyness
- anxiety
- pain
- aggression.

Some of the above indicators may be because the child has been threatened by their abuser and they are fearful that someone may find out what has occurred. Physically abused children may well cover up the abuse for fear of implications.

Physical harm can also be caused when a parent or carer deliberately induces illness in a child, for example through poisoning or by inventing or exaggerating symptoms of an illness.

Sexual abuse

If an adult uses a child for their own sexual pleasure, through either forcing them to take part in sexual activity, exposing them to pornography or indecent images or failing to protect a child against any of these things, then this is seen as sexual abuse.

Although there may be physical signs associated with sexual abuse, such as bloodstains in the underwear, pain and discomfort in the genital areas, infections, discharge and difficulties in toileting, there will also be other indicators that are not as apparent, such as behavioural and emotional problems, including:

- depression
- loneliness
- exposing themselves or masturbating
- showing signs of comfort behaviour such as sucking the thumb
- insecurity
- fear.

The child may also use their art work to give hints and clues as to what is happening to them and could be seen to 'act out' inappropriate scenarios during role play.

More often than not, sexual abuse is carried out by someone that the child knows and trusts. In many cases sexual abuse occurs during normal routines, for example at bath time or bedtime, and it may take a while for a young child to realise that anything untoward is happening to them. Many young children will simply accept the abuse and consider it 'normal'. However, when they do become aware that something is wrong, they may still keep quiet for fear of repercussion, as many abused children are threatened by their abuser and made to feel that the abuse is their own fault. It is important to remember that sexual abuse is not solely perpetrated by adult males, and women can also commit such heinous crimes. The high-profile case of nursery paedophile Vanessa George, who was jailed in 2009 for sexually assaulting young children at the nursery where she worked, is one such example. Juveniles who are children under the age of 18 years of age can also be abusers.

In 2003, the Sexual Offences Act was brought out to protect the public from sexual crime and, in particular, specific laws were brought in to protect children and families. The Act was long overdue and brought about the most significant overhaul of sexual offences legislation in more than a hundred years. Previous loopholes in the law have been addressed and new evidence regarding the patterns and impact of sexual abuse has been taken into account.

Child sexual exploitation

This is another form of sexual abuse. Child sexual exploitation is where a child is manipulated, coerced or tricked by an individual or a group of people to take part in sexual activity. Often a child is exploited in this way because the perpetrator can give them something they need, for example alcohol, drugs or money. Although the sexual activity may appear consensual, the child is still being exploited. Exploitation does not have to be through physical contact; it can occur through the use of the internet (see online abuse on page 74).

Emotional abuse

When a child is subjected to ridicule, threatening and verbal abuse and is deprived of love and affection, they are known as being emotionally abused. Emotional abuse shows little or no physical signs but the impact is widespread and extremely damaging, and the child's self-confidence will plunge, making them feel worthless. Emotionally abused children often resort to self-harm and, in severe cases, resort to suicide as a way out. They find it extremely difficult to make friends, and lasting relationships appear out of their reach as they struggle to feel accepted, loved and worthy. Emotional abuse can be very difficult to detect but some of the more common signs listed below may help to build up a bigger picture, and if a child is showing several signs then emotional abuse should be considered:

- Needing to please people all of the time, often unnecessarily.
- Showing fear in new situations and amongst new people.

- Being unable to trust people.

- Showing signs of attention-seeking.

- Telling lies.

- Regressing to wetting and soiling themselves when already toilet-trained.

- Development delays.

- Becoming aggressive.

- Showing signs of speech problems such as stuttering.

- Finding it difficult to mix with others and make friends.

- Being clingy towards one person and needing to be with them constantly.

- Stealing.

- Showing frustration and having sudden outbursts and tantrums.

Emotionally abused children are prevented from expressing their views and ideas and may be deliberately silenced, or they may be overprotected and suffer limitations on exploration and learning. A child who is made to witness the ill treatment of another person, be that another child or an adult (domestic abuse), or who is frequently left frightened or in danger is suffering from emotional abuse.

It is important to remember that some form of emotional abuse is present in *all* types of abuse but it can also occur in isolation.

Neglect

Children who do not have their basic needs met are suffering from neglect. Basic needs include food, warmth, supervision, love, education and medical care. It is difficult to understand why some children are neglected as they appear to be well loved, and in many cases neglect stems from a basic misunderstanding or lack of parenting skills or parents may be suffering from their own problems such as drug abuse or mental or physical illness. A child who is suffering from neglect will show a mixture of both physical and emotional signs. Emotional signs are similar to those listed as relating to emotional abuse above. The physical signs associated with neglect may include:

- The child needing to be bathed or washed and appearing dirty and unkempt.

- The child appearing hungry and looking underweight.

- The child wearing clothes that do not fit or that are unsuitable for the time of year.

- The child suffering from frequent accidental injuries due to a lack of supervision.

- The child suffering from toothache or minor infections, which the parent has failed to respond to and seek treatment for.

- The child regularly being tired.

- The child being left with unsuitable carers.

It is important to listen carefully to a child who is thought to be suffering from neglect, as they will often speak about being left alone or having to care for siblings. Role play and art work may give indications, and the child may appear older than their years due to the responsibilities they have, which may even include cooking and caring for parents or siblings.

Neglect can also occur in pregnancy, if the mother is a substance abuser for example.

Online abuse

Technology is used to facilitate online abuse, and social media and online games are often used to carry out this type of abuse. Harassment, bullying, threats, the sharing of indecent images of children, grooming and stalking, to name but a few, are all behaviours linked to online abuse.

Prevent duty

The Prevent duty departmental advice was published by the Department for Education in June 2015 (www.gov.uk/government/publications/prevent-duty-guidance) and explains what the Prevent duty means for schools and childcare organisations and how to demonstrate compliance. The document also contains sources of information, advice and support.

The advice states that from 1 July 2015, all registered early years childcare providers are subject to a duty under section 26 of the Counter-Terrorism and Security Act 2015 and are expected to have 'due regard to the need to prevent people from being drawn into terrorism'. This duty is known as the Prevent duty.

For any childcare professional to be able to fulfill the Prevent duty, they must first and foremost be able to identify children who may be vulnerable to radicalisation, and be confident in challenging extremist views and reporting concerns.

As outlined in the Prevent duty, there is no 'single way of identifying an individual who is likely to be susceptible to a terrorist ideology', so it is essential that staff are vigilant and alert to changes in a child's behaviour that may indicate concerns. It is the responsibility of the manager to ensure that all staff are confident and knowledgeable on this subject.

British values

The fundamental British values of democracy, rule of law, individual liberty, mutual respect and tolerance of those with different faiths and beliefs have been embedded in the Early Years Foundation Stage (EYFS) for years. Fundamental British values are specifically relevant to children's safeguarding and welfare, as they promote tolerance, respect and collaboration between individuals, allowing them to make decisions and choices whilst helping them to understand that their own behaviour and actions have consequences. Nursery managers can help to promote British values by ensuring that their staff have access to appropriate training and ensuring the setting that they manage:

- Actively helps children to appreciate and respect both their own culture and that of others.
- Promotes tolerance and respect of all faiths, cultures and races.
- Provides an environment that welcomes everyone.
- Allows children to explore similarities and differences between themselves and others, such as faith, community and tradition.
- Shares special moments and celebrations.
- Challenges stereotypes.

The examples given below are intended to demonstrate what British values mean in everyday practice.

- **Democracy** – links to personal, social and emotional development in the EYFS and focuses on self-confidence and self-awareness. It is essential that managers and staff encourage children to value each other's views and values and to ensure that children are listened to and their opinions taken into consideration.

- **Rule of law** – links to personal, social and emotional development in the EYFS and focuses on managing feelings and behaviour. Managers and staff must ensure that children understand that their actions have consequences and teach them right from wrong. Children need to learn why rules are in place and that these rules apply to everyone.

- **Individual liberty** – links to personal, social and emotional development in the EYFS and focuses on self-confidence, self-awareness and people and communities along with understanding the world. Managers and staff must provide opportunities for children to explore feelings and responsibilities and reflect on differences. They need to help to increase a child's confidence in their own abilities and develop self-knowledge.

- **Mutual respect and tolerance** – links to personal, social and emotional development in the EYFS and focuses on people and communities, managing feelings and behaviour and making relationships. Managers and staff must create an ethos of inclusivity and tolerance. The setting should value and engage in the differences in faiths, culture, views and races and encourage children to engage with the wider community. Children should be encouraged to respect, tolerate and appreciate both their own and other cultures and learn about similarities and differences.

Female genital mutilation

It is vital that all managers and staff have a very clear understanding of what female genital mutilation (FGM) is and how to spot the warning signs. Without any medical reason, the procedure is illegal and must be reported. FGM is a procedure where the girl's genitals are deliberately cut.

FGM is commonly carried out on young children up to the age of 15. The need for a strong child–practitioner bond has never been more important than in cases such as FGM, as this may lead to a disclosure. Practitioners need to respond in the same way as they would for any safeguarding disclosure and go through the appropriate recording procedures. There will be other obvious ways of identifying whether a child has been operated on in this way, such as nappy-changing time and potty training. The main signs and symptoms of this procedure include:

- difficulty in walking
- difficulty in sitting
- difficulty in standing
- prolonged periods of time spent in the bathroom
- unexplained absences of significant length from the setting
- reluctance at being changed or undressing.

If concerns are suspected or if a child has disclosed anything then it must be reported following the setting's procedures. Help and support can also be accessed anonymously from NSPCC FGM Helpline on 0800 028 3550 or by emailing fgmhelp@nspcc.org.

Managers can support practitioners in their awareness of FGM in a number of ways, such as:

- During the staff induction process when recruiting new members of staff.
- Through staff training.
- By embedding the setting's policy on FGM and making sure that all staff know how to spot the signs and symptoms and are confident reporting concerns or disclosures.

Whilst it is vital that staff are aware of the procedure and the signs and symptoms, it is equally important that they understand that they are not trained in confirming that the procedure has actually been carried out, and therefore the correct reporting procedures must be followed.

E-safety

All settings should have a policy in place to protect children in relation to electronic communications such as mobile phones and cameras.

Staff should not be permitted to use personal mobile phones whilst they are on duty and these should be switched off and kept in a secure place if brought into the workplace. Cameras should be used only to record observations of children's learning and development and the photographs should be displayed in the children's files.

Whilst the internet is now regarded as an essential resource for supporting teaching and learning, appropriate software and filters must be in place to protect children.

E-mails should be password-protected and monitored by the manager.

Social media should also be monitored by the manager and policies put in place preventing staff from discussing any work issues on sites such as Facebook. It should be made clear to staff that any work-related issues or material that could identify an individual who is a child, parent, relative or work colleague, which could adversely affect any of the same, or the setting, must not be placed on a social networking site.

Exercise

Spend some time looking at the social media profile pages of your staff team. Are the visible posts acceptable for a person working with young children? Are any of the posts offensive or discriminatory? Do they mention the workplace? Can they be construed as being detrimental to the business? Dependent upon your findings, consider the action you will need to take to remove any offending posts and prevent similar situations occurring again.

Staff behaviour

Clear policies and procedures should be set out with regard to acceptable behaviour in the workplace. Personal harassment and peer-on-peer abuse should never be tolerated and staff should be encouraged to be polite and courteous at all times. Rudeness must not be tolerated towards fellow colleagues, children, families or visitors and it should be made clear to staff that they are expected to use their best endeavours to promote the interests of the setting at all times. Managers should lead by example at all times.

Whilst it is not always possible to monitor staff behaviour outside the workplace, managers should make it clear that staff are expected to act with the highest integrity during work time and maintain these standards outside of working hours too.

Policies and procedures

A robust set of policies and procedures must be in place to cover the safeguarding and welfare of children, families and staff in the setting. It is, however, equally important that all staff have read the policies and that they understand them. Policies and procedures need to cover all the main areas of the provision and set out what is expected of individuals with no room for ambiguity.

It is essential that managers are aware of how well informed their staff are with regard to all aspects of safeguarding. These issues should be discussed when carrying out supervisions, and any training needs should be identified at that time. However, it is good practice for managers to ask themselves some important questions periodically in order that they are completely aware of how well informed their staff team are. A simple self-assessment questionnaire like the one below could help to identify any weaknesses in your setting.

1. How well informed is the designated safeguarding officer about safeguarding and child protection issues?
2. How well informed are the entire staff team with regard to safeguarding issues?
3. When was the last time the safeguarding policy was reviewed and updated?
4. Are the safeguarding policy and procedures effective? How do you know?
5. Are staff inductions effective and do they support staff's knowledge of child protection and safeguarding?
6. Are you confident that all your staff can spot the signs of abuse?
7. Are you confident that all your staff know the procedures for reporting suspicions of abuse?
8. Does your setting's continuing professional development programme support child protection and safeguarding?
9. Are your safeguarding practices shared with everyone involved in the setting, including parents and visitors?

Your answers to the above questions will help you to ascertain which areas are secure and which require more training.

Chapter 5
Health and safety

The Statutory Framework for the Early Years Foundation Stage (Department for Education, 2017) is mandatory for all early years providers in England, maintained schools, non-maintained schools, independent schools, all providers on the Early Years Register and all providers registered with an early years childminder agency. The updated framework, which came into force in April 2017, refers to the following legislation:

- The learning and development requirements under section 39 (1)(a) of the Childcare Act 2006.

- The safeguarding and welfare requirements under section 39 (1(b) of the Childcare Act 2006.

The Statutory Framework states that it is mandatory for providers to take all necessary steps to keep children safe and well, and this covers a number of areas such as child protection, suitability of staff and the safety and suitability of premises, environment and equipment.

In every nursery, policies and procedures should be in place relating to all matters of health and safety, and in this chapter we will look at some key areas, including illness, first aid, food hygiene, cleanliness and maintenance of the setting, and risk assessments. As nursery manager, it is your responsibility to ensure that you and your staff adhere to these policies at all times to ensure the safety of the children in your care.

Health and safety legislation is constantly being updated as knowledge and research into accident prevention and health and safety issues increase, and it is therefore vital that the manager of a setting ensures that they keep abreast of these updates. This can be done in a number of ways, such as through training and signing up to receive updates from Ofsted and other organisations in the industry.

Illness

It is essential that all providers promote the good health of everyone attending the setting, including children and staff. Policies should be in place, and discussed with parents and staff, outlining the procedures that must be followed if children are ill or infectious. Likewise there must be effective policies and procedures in place for administering medication.

There may be times when a sick child is in the setting. This situation could come about because the child has become ill during the course of the day whilst they are in your care, or they may have been brought to the setting that morning suffering from an illness either that has got worse during the day or that the parent has failed to inform you of.

Childcare practitioners are not obliged to care for sick children and the manager must use their own discretion, and the setting's policies and procedures, when deciding whether a child is too ill to be in the setting. When making your mind up you should base your decision on:

- The presence of any other children and whether the sick child poses a threat to their health.
- Your own health and that of colleagues, and whether the sick child poses any risk to staff.
- The child themselves – if they are clearly unwell and are not enjoying being in the setting then their parents should be informed.

Settings should have a policy regarding caring for sick children. Although most parents will put the welfare of their children first and would not expect you to care for their child when they are clearly unwell, you may also come across parents who, with no back-up cover of their own, may find it difficult to get time off work when their children are ill and may take advantage of your good nature and bring their children to the setting when they are clearly not well enough to be there.

A sick child policy may look something like this:

PROMOTING HEALTH AND HYGIENE

Managing children with allergies or who are sick or infectious (including reporting notifiable diseases).

Policy statement

We provide care for healthy children and promote health through identifying allergies and preventing contact with the allergenic substance and through preventing cross-infection of viruses and bacterial infections.

Procedures for children with allergies

- When parents start their children at the setting they are asked if their child suffers from any known allergies. This is recorded on the registration form.
- If a child has an allergy, a risk assessment form is completed to detail the following:
    - The allergen, i.e. the substance, material or living creature the child is allergic to, such as nuts, eggs, bee stings, cats, etc.
    - The nature of the allergic reactions, e.g. anaphylactic shock reaction, including rash, reddening of skin, swelling, breathing problems, etc.
    - What to do in case of allergic reactions, any medication used and how it is to be used, e.g. EpiPen®.
    - Control measures – such as how the child can be prevented from contact with the allergen.
- The review form is kept in the child's personal file and a copy is displayed where staff can see it.
- Parents train staff in how to administer special medication in the event of an allergic reaction.
- Generally, no nuts or nut products are used within the setting.
- Parents are made aware so that no nut or nut products are accidentally brought in, for example to a party.

Insurance requirements for children with allergies and disabilities

- The insurance will automatically include children with any disability or allergy but certain procedures must be strictly adhered to, as set out below. For children suffering life threatening conditions, or requiring invasive treatments, written confirmation from your insurance provider must be obtained to extend the insurance.

At all times the administration of medication must be compliant with the welfare requirements of the Early Years Foundation Stage.

Oral medication

Asthma inhalers are now regarded as 'oral medication' by insurers and so documents do not need to be forwarded to your insurance provider.

- Oral medications must be prescribed by a GP or have manufacturer's instructions clearly written on them.
- The group must be provided with clear written instructions on how to administer such medication.
- All risk assessment procedures need to be adhered to for the correct storage and administration of the medication.
- The group must have the parent's or guardian's prior written consent. This consent must be kept on file. It is not necessary to forward copy documents to your insurance provider.

Life-saving medication and invasive treatments

This includes adrenaline injections (EpiPens®) for anaphylactic shock reactions (caused by allergies to nuts, eggs, etc.) or invasive treatments such as rectal administration of Diazepam (for epilepsy).

The setting must have:

- A letter from the child's GP or consultant stating the child's condition and what medication if any is to be administered.
- Written consent from the parent or guardian allowing staff to administer medication.
- Proof of training in the administration of such medication by the child's GP, a district nurse, a children's nurse specialist or a community paediatric nurse.

There must be a key person for special needs children – children requiring assistance with tubes to help them with everyday living, e.g. breathing apparatus, to take nourishment, colostomy bags, etc.

- Prior written consent is required from the child's parent or guardian to give treatment and/or medication prescribed by the child's GP.
- The key person must have the relevant medical training or experience, which may include those who have received appropriate instructions from parents or guardians, or who have qualifications.

Procedures for children who are sick or infectious

- If children appear unwell during the day – have a temperature, sickness, diarrhoea or pains, particularly in the head or stomach – the manager or room leader calls the parents and asks them to collect the child or send a known carer to collect them on their behalf.
- If a child has a temperature, they are kept cool, by removing top clothing and sponging their heads with cool water, but are kept away from draughts.
- Temperature is taken using a 'fever scan' kept near to the first aid box.
- In extreme cases of emergency the child should be taken to the nearest hospital and the parent informed.
- Parents are asked to take their child to the doctor before returning them to nursery; the nursery can refuse admittance to children who have a temperature, sickness and diarrhoea or a contagious infection or disease.
- Where children have been prescribed antibiotics, parents are asked to keep them at home for 48 hours before returning to the setting.
- After diarrhoea, parents are asked to keep children home for 48 hours or until a formed stool is passed.
- The setting has a list of excludable diseases and current exclusion times. The full list is obtainable from www.publichealth.hscni.net (Northern Ireland) and includes common childhood illnesses such as measles. This list is also displayed on the office wall.

Reporting of 'notifiable diseases'

- If a child or adult is diagnosed as suffering from a notifiable disease under the Public Health (Infectious Diseases) Regulations 1988, the GP will report this to the Health Protection Agency.
- When the setting becomes aware or is formally informed of the notifiable disease, the manager informs Ofsted and acts on any advice given by the Health Protection Agency.

Guidance on Infection Control in Schools and other Childcare Settings, which sets out when and for how long children need to be excluded from settings, when treatment/medication is required and where to get further advice, can be found at www.publichealth.hscni.net (Northern Ireland).

HIV/hepatitis procedure

- HIV virus, like other viruses such as hepatitis (A, B and C), is spread through body fluids. Hygiene precautions for dealing with body fluids are the same for all children and adults.
- Single-use vinyl gloves and aprons are worn when changing children's nappies, pants and clothing that are soiled with blood, urine, faeces or vomit.
- Protective rubber gloves are used for cleaning and sluicing clothing after changing.
- Soiled clothing is rinsed and either bagged for parents to collect or laundered in the nursery.
- Spills of blood, urine, faeces or vomit are cleared using mild disinfectant solution and mops; cloths used are disposed of with the clinical waste.
- Tables and other furniture, furnishings or toys affected by blood, urine, faeces or vomit are cleaned using a disinfectant.
- Children do not share toothbrushes, which are also soaked weekly in sterilising solution.

Nits and head lice

- Nits and head lice are not an excludable condition, although in exceptional cases a parent may be asked to keep the child away until the infestation has cleared.
- On identifying cases of head lice, all parents are informed and asked to treat their child and all the family if they are found to have head lice.

First aid

The Statutory Framework for the Early Years Foundation Stage (Department for Education, 2017) states that 'at least one person who has a current paediatric first aid certificate must be on the premises and available at all times when children are present'. The nursery manager is responsible for ensuring that they have sufficient numbers of qualified first aiders amongst their staff in order to adhere to this requirement, and for arranging training for further staff members if not. The manager must ensure that first aid training is carried out by a regulated provider such as St John's Ambulance or the British Red Cross and that the training is renewed every three years. Whilst the framework states that only one person with first aid training must be present and available at all times, it is good practice to have more qualified first aiders, and indeed many settings insist that all practitioners are trained in first aid.

In fact, the framework also states that 'all newly qualified entrants to the early years workforce who have completed a level 2 and/or level 3 qualification on or after 30 June 2016 must also have completed either a full PFA [paediatric first aid training] or an emergency PFA certificate within three months of starting work in order to be included in the required staff:child ratios at level 2 or 3 in an early years setting'.

Exercise

What percentage of your staff currently hold a valid first aid certificate? Of those who hold the certificate, how many are on the premises at any one time? If you have a limited number of qualified first aiders, how do you manage staffing to ensure that at least one qualified first aider is on the premises at all times and how does this affect holiday and illness cover? After researching this information, do you feel you need to arrange for more members of staff to be trained in first aid?

Criteria for effective paediatric first aid training

According to the framework (Department for Education, 2017), it is essential that the paediatric first aid training that staff enrol on 'is designed for workers caring for young children in the absence of their parents and is appropriate to the age of the children being cared for'. A certificate must be obtained following training as proof of competence and the certificate must be renewed every three years.

The framework states that a full paediatric first aid course should last for a minimum of 12 hours (excluding any breaks) and cover the following areas:

- Understanding the role and responsibilities of the paediatric first aider, including the appropriate contents of a first aid box and the need for recording accidents and incidents.
- Assessing an emergency situation and prioritising what action needs to be taken.
- Helping a baby or child:
  - who is unresponsive and breathing normally
  - who is unresponsive and not breathing normally
  - who is having a seizure
  - who is choking
  - who is bleeding
  - who is suffering from shock caused by severe blood loss
  - who is suffering from anaphylactic shock
  - who has had an electric shock
  - who has burns or scalds
  - who has a suspected fracture
  - with head, neck or back injuries
  - who is suspected of being poisoned
  - with a foreign body in eyes, ears or nose
  - with an eye injury
  - with a bite or sting
  - who is suffering from the effects of extreme heat or cold
  - having a diabetic emergency, an asthma attack, an allergic reaction, meningitis, febrile convulsions. (Department for Education, 2017)

The framework also stipulates that an emergency paediatric first aid course should be undertaken face-to-face and last for a minimum of six hours (excluding any breaks) and cover the following areas:

- Being able to assess an emergency situation and prioritising what action needs to be taken.
- Helping a baby or child:
  - who is unresponsive and breathing normally
  - who is unresponsive and not breathing normally
  - who is having a seizure
  - who is choking
  - who is bleeding
  - who is suffering from shock caused by severe blood loss. (Department for Education, 2017)

The nursery manager is responsible for ensuring that any first aid training they arrange for their staff adheres to this criteria. They should also decide whether annual refresher courses are relevant in addition to renewing the certificate every three years in order to keep abreast of any changes to procedures and to maintain basic skills.

Food hygiene

You may be quite surprised to learn some of the facts associated with food hygiene and these may help you to understand why, as a nursery leader, you must take food safety very seriously and ensure that your staff do the same.

It makes sense therefore to look at some of the more serious consequences of getting things wrong when it comes to food safety. What might happen? What might be the consequences to you and the setting you are managing?

- Your setting may be the cause of infecting someone with food poisoning, which could result in that person becoming ill or, in more serious cases, cause death.

FACT!	FACT!	FACT!
Washing hands effectively should take at least 20 seconds.	Use-by dates should be respected even if food looks and smells fine.	Fridge temperatures should be kept below five degrees Celsius.

FACT!	FACT!
Food that is not going to be consumed immediately should be cooled quickly, within 90 minutes, and then stored in either a fridge or a freezer.	Raw meat, including poultry, should NOT be washed before cooking, as this can spread bacteria around the kitchen. Bacteria will be killed upon cooking correctly.

Figure 5.1 Health and safety facts
Source: www.nhs.uk

- You, as the manager, are likely to have dissatisfied customers and a lot of complaints.

- Your setting's reputation will suffer and this may lead to a loss of business, which will have a 'knock-on' effect towards job losses and potential closure of the business.

- Your setting's costs may escalate if the business is faced with paying fines or replacing contaminated food supplies.

All businesses serving food should be registered appropriately. In order to assist customers to choose food outlets that have passed rigorous tests, the UK operates a number of food hygiene rating schemes, which provide customers with information relating to the inspection of the business premises and food handling practices.

Nursery businesses should contact their local authority to register their business at least 28 days before opening. The local authority will inspect the premises to ensure that the design and construction meets legal requirements. Once approval has been granted, unannounced inspections will take place annually to ensure the General Food Law Requirements are being upheld. A new rating will be awarded following each inspection and this will reflect the level of hygiene found on the day of the inspection.

The nursery manager will be responsible for ensuring that the nursery cook follows the General Food Law Requirements, is up to date with food hygiene training and completes all relevant paperwork. The

Figure 5.2 A level 5 rating for food hygiene under the FHRS and a pass under the FHIS
Source: The Food Standards Agency, © Crown Copyright.

manager is also responsible for sourcing suitable food hygiene training for all staff who handle food, including those who prepare snacks.

The Food Standards Agency (FSA) was established in April 2000. Its aim is to protect the health of the public in relation to food. It is the job of the FSA to provide information and assistance to businesses including those in the food industry, enforcers and consumers themselves.

The FSA runs the Food Hygiene Rating Scheme (FHRS) in partnership with local authorities in England, Wales and Northern Ireland. This is a six-level scoring system starting with zero for very poor quality through to a five for very good quality. This scoring system is used in the UK.

Similarly, the Food Hygiene Information System (FHIS) is a two-level scoring system that rates hygiene standards against legal requirements in Scotland. The grades are either 'pass' or 'improvement required'. Scotland also has a separate scheme called the 'Eat Safe Award', which recognises businesses that achieve over and above what is legally expected of them.

The laws relating to food businesses in the UK

The Food Hygiene (England) Regulations 2006 (along with similar legislation in Scotland, Wales and Northern Ireland) bring the European regulations listed below into the UK national law. In addition to this, the legislation also:

- Updates previous food safety laws.
- Strengthens existing legal powers and penalties.
- Sets specific UK temperature control requirements.

The Regulation (EC) No 852/2004 on the hygiene of foodstuffs is a European law that lays down the general principles and requirements of food laws in European Union countries. This law requires all food businesses to:

- Register with their local authority.
- Document food safety procedures and keep appropriate records.
- Follow general food hygiene requirements.
- Comply with temperature control requirements for foodstuffs.
- Provide the necessary food training and hygiene training to all food handlers.
- Operate a food safety management system that is based on the principles of hazard analysis and critical control points (HACCP).

The Food Safety Act 1990 is an amended act that provides the framework for food legislation in Great Britain. Northern Ireland follows similar legislation and the law covers:

- False or misleading information regarding the description of food.
- Supplying food that is harmful to health.
- Providing food that is not of a suitable nature, quality or substance expected by customers.
- Possessing for the purpose of sale or selling food that does not comply with the food safety standards.

As a nursery manager, it is paramount that you are aware of the legislation surrounding food hygiene and the policies and procedures you must put in place in order to protect your business and the children in your care. The list below, although not exhaustive, gives an idea of some of the precautions you could take:

- robust record-keeping
- inspection of all deliveries received
- suitable pest control
- robust cleaning schedules, which are adhered to at all times
- staff training
- exceptionally high standards of personal hygiene.

These precautions could also be used in defence of legal action in relation to food safety and hygiene should this be required. If a business can prove that they have taken every reasonable precaution to ensure the safety of the food they prepare and serve then the company may be successful in their defence of a claim. Despite rigorous systems being in place, there may still be a small percentage of the time when a business is accused of breaking the law, but by exercising 'due diligence' it should be possible to show that the offence was the fault of another person rather than the business owner. For example, a food handler working in a business could be prosecuted if they have ignored company rules or have been negligent, rather than the business owner themselves. However, it is important to remember that any cases of food hygiene against a business will be detrimental, and therefore all measures should be taken to ensure that negligence is avoided. As a manager, you have a duty to ensure that employees are aware of, and abide by, the company rules.

Exercise

Look carefully at which members of staff, in addition to the nursery cook, prepare and serve food. Do your practitioners prepare snacks? If so, are these members of staff suitably qualified? ALL members of staff who prepare meals or snacks should hold an up-to-date food hygiene certificate.

Environmental health practitioners

What are environmental health practitioners and what rights have they got? Environmental health practitioners were formerly known as environmental health officers or EHOs for short. They have the right to enter any establishment selling food, at any reasonable time, in order to inspect the premises, food, equipment and the procedures being followed. If you do not allow the environmental health practitioner to enter the premises you will be obstructing the law, so you must allow them entry to inspect your nursery if requested. During an inspection, the environmental health practitioner may request swabs taken from work surfaces, food samples and written records in order for them to make a reasonable and accurate judgement of the premises, equipment and food.

Cleanliness of the setting

In order to maintain high standards and promote healthy outcomes for children, it is imperative that the setting is kept clean and free from the risk of infection. This can only be done if effective systems are put in place and regularly monitored. Tidying up throughout the day and instilling in both staff and children the importance of using toys and equipment in a respectful manner will help to maintain a building and contents that are fit for purpose.

It will be necessary to have effective cleaning procedures in place and the manager should ensure that these schedules are up to date and maintained. It is important to bear in mind how many people will be using the setting on a daily basis and, in order to ensure that the environment is risk-free, regular sanitising of toys and equipment is essential to avoid cross-infection.

Whilst many large settings might employ a cleaner to take care of the routine cleaning, it is essential that all staff are aware of how to deal with toileting accidents or when a child is sick. Set routines should be in place for tidying up and cleaning all areas, including floors, walls, resources, furniture and equipment.

All staff should be good role models when promoting personal hygiene and provide good examples of how to maintain a safe and hygienic indoor and outdoor environment.

Request that your staff adhere to the following guidelines to promote personal hygiene:

- Staff should ensure that they turn up for work every day looking clean and smart. This includes clean hair, skin, teeth and clothes.

As a manager you should be prepared to confront any member of staff who does not conform to the company's expected dress code or look suitable to carry out their role.

- Staff should be seen to wash their hands regularly and they must promote the same for the children. Hands should be washed before eating and after using the toilet, blowing noses, playing outside, and so forth.

- Staff must be provided with disposable gloves and aprons for use when changing nappies or dealing with blood, faeces, urine and vomit and the manager must ensure that these are well stocked and used.

- Long hair should be tied back.

- Nails should be kept short, and any staff who prepare food or snacks should either wear protective gloves or ensure that they do not wear nail varnish.

- Jewellery should be avoided.

- Cuts and sores should be covered.

Maintenance

Whilst it may not necessarily be the manager's job to carry out maintenance, it will be their responsibility to report damages and arrange for any necessary maintenance to be carried out, and therefore it is essential that procedures are put in place that ensure all staff are aware of how to report breakages or damaged equipment and resources in order that effective measures can be put in place to reduce accidents and assess risks.

It is a good idea for the setting to have a health and safety book that is easily accessible to everyone. Staff should be encouraged to note down, in the book, any risks they have seen, in addition to reporting them to the manager. This will mean a secondary check is in place – the book should be signed when the risk has been eliminated.

Routine maintenance checks should be in place and the manager should be checking for routine wear and tear on toys and equipment and encouraging staff to do the same.

Risk assessments

All settings need to carry out regular risk assessments and all staff must be competent in recognising and reducing any potential risks. It is important to understand the difference between a hazard and a risk:

* Hazard – this is the source of potential harm.
* Risk – this is the possibility of potential harm.

A risk assessment is done to identify the hazard and ascertain how to overcome or reduce it.

All settings must have risk assessments in place to cover all potential hazards. An effective assessment will take into account the hazard, the potential for something to go wrong and how it can be reduced or prevented. It should take into account who is at risk and evaluate the likelihood of injury. Risk assessments must be regularly monitored and reviewed by the manager in order for them to be effective.

Risk assessments should be in place for both children and staff. All settings should be aware of the necessary risk assessments for children, such as checking doors, gates and windows, routinely checking play equipment, ensuring that sand pits are covered when not in use, ensuring safe storage of equipment such as scissors and knives, ensuring that water is not left unattended in buckets, bowls, trays, and so forth. However, not all settings will have additional risk assessments in place that solely refer to staff, such as pregnant women in the workplace, safe lifting, moving and handling, and display screen equipment (DSE). It is good practice for managers to identify risks to the health and safety of everyone in the setting, not just the children, and ensure that risk assessments are in place.

Some of the risk assessments that you may like to put in place include:

* display screens
* work-related stress – this can be used when dealing with issues such as staff wellbeing covered in Chapter 3, page 56
* working alone

- violence and threatening behaviour – from both children and parents.

Below are some examples of risk assessments that could be used in the setting for pregnant employees and those using DSE on a regular basis – such as administration staff and management. You will find printable versions of these forms at www.bloomsbury.com/outstanding-nursery-leader.

RISK ASSESSMENT CHECKLIST: NEW AND EXPECTANT MOTHERS		
AREA OF ASSESSMENT	YES/NO	COMMENT
Does the job involve twisting/ stooping/lifting/stretching?		
Does the woman have to stand or sit for long periods of time without a break?		
Is protective equipment (aprons etc.) provided in suitable sizes?		
If uniforms are obligatory, are they provided in maternity sizes and comfortable for pregnant employees to wear?		
Are there any infection risks in the work such as clearing up body fluids? If so, are adequate hygiene precautions in place?		
Does the employee have any flexibility over working hours?		
Are there any parts of the job that may be particularly stressful?		
Are colleagues and supervisors supportive towards pregnant workers?		
Does the employee have any concerns about her own pregnancy?		

Are there arrangements for sufficient breaks and access to hot/cold drinks?		
Is there somewhere quiet for pregnant workers to rest or lie down?		
Is there a clean, private area to express and store breast milk?		
Manager's comments		
Questionnaire completed by		
Date		

SELF-ASSESSMENT QUESTIONNAIRE: STAFF USING DISPLAY SCREEN EQUIPMENT (DSE)		
DSE USE	YES/NO	COMMENTS
Are you required to use DSE for work on a daily basis?		
Do you use DSE for more than one hour per day continuously?		
Is the screen located in front of you when using the unit?		
Can the screen be tilted or adjusted to ensure a comfortable position?		
Can the keyboard be positioned so that it is comfortable to use?		
Is there sufficient space for wrists to rest when not using the keyboard?		

Is the mouse easy to access, with adequate space to manoeuvre?		
Is the keyboard clear and easy to use?		
Is the height of the chair adjustable?		
Can the backrest of the chair be adjusted and tilted?		
Is the chair fitted with arms that can be positioned to suit posture?		
Does the desk give adequate workspace to allow easy use of the screen, keyboard and mouse?		
Is the area adequately lit?		
When positioned to use the keyboard are your upper arms in line with your upper body?		
With your fingers on the keys are your wrists straight?		
When in this position is your back adequately supported by the chair's backrest?		
Have you had your eyes tested for use with DSE?		

Have you ever suffered from work-related aches or pains in your: • wrists • forearms • neck • eyes • back?		
Have you ever suffered from epilepsy?		
Manager's comments		
Questionnaire completed by		
Date		

Accidents, incidents and pre-existing injuries

It is paramount that all early years settings follow the guidelines of RIDDOR (reporting of injuries, diseases and dangerous occurrences regulations) when reporting accidents and incidents. The law specifies that every workplace must have an accident report book, which must be easily accessible to staff and volunteers, and it must be explained to them how the book is to be completed. All accidents should be regularly reviewed to see whether any patterns arise and how best any potential problems can be reduced. Information recorded in the accident book must include:

- The name of the person who has sustained the injury.
- The date the injury happened.
- The time the injury happened.
- The location where the injury happened.
- An exact account of what happened.
- A description of the injury sustained.
- What treatment was given.

- The name and signature of the person dealing with the accident.
- The name and signature of the person who witnessed the accident.
- In the case of a child, the signature of the parent or carer to show that they have been informed of the accident.

The safeguarding and welfare requirements in the Statutory Framework for the Early Years Foundation Stage (Department for Education, 2017) clearly state that providers must notify Ofsted when the following incidents occur:

- An outbreak of food poisoning that affects two or more children on the premises.
- Any injury that requires treatment by a GP or hospital doctor.
- The death of a child or adult (this should be done as soon as possible but certainly within 14 days of the incident occurring).

In order for settings to comply with RIDDOR, a report must be submitted to the Health and Safety Executive if:

- Any accident occurs to a member of staff resulting in treatment by a GP or hospital.
- There is any dangerous occurrence such as a gas leak.

All settings must keep reports of any incidents occurring on the premises such as:

- burglary
- intruders gaining access without authorisation
- attacks on any members of staff or parents
- flood, fire, electrical failure or gas leak
- death of a child
- racist incidents involving staff or families
- terrorist attack or the threat of one.

Each of the above incidents must be recorded along with the date and time of the incident and a full account of the incident, including the names of those affected and any action that was taken, for example reporting the incident to the police.

All early years settings have a responsibility under the requirements of the Statutory Framework for the Early Years Foundation Stage to keep children safe and promote their welfare, and there are certain forms relating to health and safety that must be kept on the premises. These forms include the accident form, the pre-existing injury form, the medication form and the treatment record form.

Accident form

This form is used to record any accident or injury that a child may sustain whilst in the setting or during any outings arranged by the provider. The form should be completed in duplicate, with the copy given to the parent or carer and the original kept in the child's personal file. The accident form should include the nature of the injury, the treatment given or action taken and the name of the person who dealt with the accident. The date and time should be included and the report should be accurate, detailed and legible. An accident form should look something like the following example. A printable version of this form is available at www. bloomsbury.com/outstanding-nursery-leader.

ACCIDENT FORM				
Date				
Who was involved in the accident? *(Please circle)*	Child Adult Member of staff			
Name				
Date of birth				
Date of accident				
Time of accident				
Place accident occurred				
Explain fully the events leading up to the accident and the accident itself	Slip	Trip	Fall	Other

Size of injury				
Witnessed by				
Position and type of injury	Give details of size of injury and mark on body map FRONT BACK			
Give details of further medical treatment required? *Contact the parent immediately if the accident has resulted in a head injury or if further medical treatment is required.*	Observation	Compress	Medical	Other
Is there anything we could do to prevent this happening again? If yes, give details	Yes	No	Details	

Is a piece of furniture/ resource/toy at fault?	Furniture	Toy	Resource
If yes, should it be removed? Give details			
Witness signature			
Staff signature			
Manager signature			
Parent signature			

Pre-existing injury form

This form should be completed by the parent/carer to inform the setting of any injuries sustained by a child outside of the setting. The form will look something like the example below. A printable version of this form is available at www.bloomsbury.com/outstanding-nursery-leader.

PRE-EXISTING INJURY

- Child's name...
- Date of birth.....................................
- Date in nursery..
- Date of accident ....
- Type of accident...
  ....
- ....
  ....
- ....
  ....
- Injury (any cuts or bruises) ....
  ....
- ....
  ....
- Please identify the area of injury

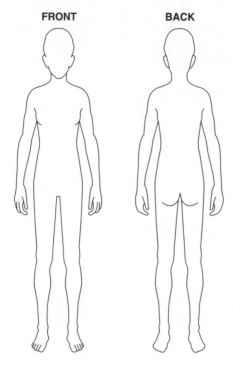

- **Signature of parent** ....
- **Signature of staff member** ....

Note: We are legally required to keep a record of any injuries the child comes to nursery with. All the information given on this slip is confidential and will be kept as such.

Medication and treatment record forms

The medication form is used to record any short-term medicine a child may require. The form should be signed by both the parent and the member of staff who administers the medicine. The form should also include a section for the parent to complete, giving details of any medicine they have administered to the child prior to coming into the setting. Some providers have separate forms for parent-administered medication.

The treatment record form is used to record long-term treatments such as an inhaler to treat asthma.

Chapter 6
Observation, assessment and planning

The Statutory Framework for the Early Years Foundation Stage (Department for Education, 2017) gives a clear indication of the importance of assessment in recognising the progress made by children and why accurate assessment plays an important part in understanding the needs of children and planning for these needs.

Ongoing assessment, which is also known as formative assessment, is the process of observing children in order to understand their current level of achievement, interests and the way in which they learn, and then using this information to plan for their future learning experiences.

Whilst necessary, observations and assessments on children have been heavily criticised, not least because of the time it takes to carry out these crucial checks, and many practitioners complain that spending time carrying out observations and assessments takes them away from being with the children. Managers need to understand these frustrations and plan time for staff to carry out these essential tasks associated with their jobs whilst making sure that the time they spend with the children is not compromised.

The Department for Education have also recognised that paperwork can be burdensome and the statutory framework does not dictate how paperwork must be done, leaving this to the discretion of each setting and allowing them to develop a system that works for them:

Assessment should not entail prolonged breaks from interaction with children, nor require excessive paperwork. Paperwork should be limited to that which is absolutely necessary to promote children's successful learning and development.

The framework does, however, go on to state: 'Parents and/or carers should be kept up-to-date with their child's progress and development.' (Department for Education, 2017; section 2.2, page 13)

There are many ways in which settings can demonstrate how they observe and assess children, and this can be done through written paperwork and logged in a journal for each child or, as is the case for many settings now, through an online system whereby practitioners can assess, track and document children's learning through a system that has been developed for this purpose.

Many local authorities produce their own online tracking systems, although private companies can also offer packages and bespoke services for nursery settings. The main advantage of online systems is that they allow practitioners to input data, which can then be viewed by management in order to study the progress of children both individually and collectively throughout the setting. These systems are particularly helpful when looking at progress in different 'groups', as data can be analysed depending on certain areas, such as the progress of boys in writing between the ages of three and five or the emotional progress made by all the children in the toddler room. By analysing data in this way, managers can see at a glance whether there are any problems that need to be addressed and, if so, how best to address them. It may be, for example, that the majority of the boys in the pre-school room appear to be slightly behind with their writing, and the manager can then look closely at why this might be the case. Is there a lack of suitable resources? Are the boys not being suitably engaged? Are their interests not being followed? Do the staff require further training in this area?

Knowing how to assess

Practitioners need to know children well before they can begin to assess their development, and it is for this reason that many settings do not begin to assess children's development until after they have settled into the nursery, perhaps after about six weeks. By delaying the assessment process until the child has settled properly, practitioners can get to know them, understand their likes and dislikes and plan activities around their interests, enabling the child to become at ease, and a true reflection of their achievements and progress can be seen.

When assessing children's progress we are making judgements about what the observations we have carried out are telling us in terms of the child's development, learning, health and wellbeing. It is important that the nursery manager ensures all practitioners are trained in carrying out appropriate and effective observations and assessments in the setting. This includes a baseline assessment when the child first enrols in the nursery, as well as regular observations of the child during their time in the setting.

Baseline assessments

When a child is first enrolled into the nursery, a baseline assessment may be carried out with the child's parents or carers. This will give the practitioner a 'starting point' and help to provide a picture of where the child is currently in terms of development. The baseline assessment will show the child's likes and interests and highlight any potential problems or delays in development. It is worth remembering, when collecting information from parents or carers, that sometimes they will have little, if anything, to make comparisons with and may not be aware of developmental delays. Therefore practitioners need to be sensitive when carrying out baseline assessments with parents or carers. Baseline assessments need not be complex and often settings will call them something less formal. The assessment can be done formally through the completion of an assessment form or informally via a chat with the child's parent or carer and note-taking. Some settings will use the Early Years Foundation Stage tracking sheet. See page 108 for an example of this and download a printable version at www.bloomsbury.com/outstanding-nursery-leader.

EYFS TRACKING SHEET

Name	Setting	
Date of birth	Key person	Start date

Area of learning		0–11	8–20	16–26	22–36	30–50	40–60+
Personal, social and emotional	Making relationships						
	Self-confidence and self awareness						
	Managing feelings and behaviour						
Communication and language	Listening and attention						
	Understanding						
	Speaking						
Physical	Moving and handling						
Literacy	Health and self-care						
	Reading						
	Writing		■	■			
Mathematics	Numbers						
	Shape, space and measure	■					
Understanding the world	People and communities	■	■				
	The world						
Expressive art and design	Technology	■	■				
	Exploring media and materials	■					
	Being imaginative	■	■				

■ There are no development matters statements for this age range.

The parent should identify what their child can do with reference to the Early Years Foundation Stage framework, and that section should be colour-coded and labelled in the bottom section as parental input and then dated. This can then be used for the practitioner to base their initial assessment of the child and can be developed as and when the child progresses and the practitioner assesses this progress.

Carrying out effective observations

When carrying out an observation of a child, practitioners need to make sure that the child is placed firmly at the centre of the process. Observations must be accurate, current and impartial.

When observing children, we are closely watching and listening to them and taking careful notice of what they are doing whilst recording our findings accurately. Practitioners must remain focused when carrying out observations and must not make assumptions or draw their own conclusions.

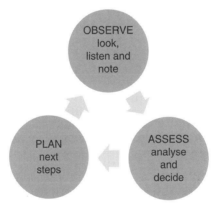

Figure 6.1 The process of observation – assessment – planning

Figure 6.1 shows the three simple steps that practitioners need to follow when assessing children:

- Observe – this is the time when the practitioner watches and listens to the child whilst making impartial notes.

- Assess – this is the time when the practitioner analyses their observation and decides what it tells them about the child.

- Plan – this is the time when the practitioner considers the child's next steps, planning for their experiences, opportunities and interests using the learning environment, resources and routines, and taking into account their own role in the child's development.

When carrying out an observation on a child, it is vital that the practitioner is *objective*. Being able to assess objectively is not always easy and it is a skill that needs to be developed. In order to be able to observe in an anti-discriminatory and anti-biased way, practitioners need to be able to observe a child without having any preconceived ideas. Having the ability to observe without relying on personal prejudices is not always an easy task but, in order for our observations to be accurate and meaningful rather than preconceived and subjective, this skill must be mastered. Managers will need to ensure that the whole team understands how to observe, assess and plan for the children and that they are doing this consistently throughout the setting.

Below is an example of a long observation carried out on a baby. You will find a blank, printable version of this form at www.bloomsbury.com/outstanding-nursery-leader.

LONG OBSERVATION FORM		
Name: A Baby	Date: 7th August 2017	Time: 9.30am – 9.55am
Age in months: 14 months	Key person: A Practitioner	Completed by: A Practitioner

Observation
'A' explores the sand in the tray with confidence. He picks up a small rake with his right hand and scrapes the sand to create marks. He moves the sand around the tray with his rake and pats it with his left hand. As he pats the sand, 'A' looks at the sand on his hand. He scrunches his fingers together to explore the texture. He then sits on the floor holding a bucket in his left hand and a scoop in his right. He sits for a few seconds and taps the bucket with the scoop.

'A' kneels in front of the tray and pats the scoop in the sand. He then pulls himself back up to stand and continues to explore the sand. He enjoys tapping his scoop on the tray then on the bucket. He repeats this action several times as he plays in the sand. After a few minutes he crouches down and crawls away from the sand tray.

Next steps
'A' is highly involved in this activity. He explores the sand tray with confidence. He enjoys combining objects. I plan to encourage him to explore a wide variety of materials.

Areas of learning covered (prime and specific)		
PSED	Making relationships	Self-confidence and self-esteem	Managing feelings and behaviour
CL	Listening and attention	Understanding	Speaking
PD	Moving and handling		Health and self-care
LIT	Reading		Writing
MATH	Numbers		Shape, space and measure
UTW	People and communities	The world	Technology
EAD	Exploring and using media and materials		Being imaginative
Characteristics of effective learning		
Playing and exploring	Active learning	Creating and thinking critically
Finding out and exploring	Being involved and concentrating	Having their own ideas
Play with what they know	Keeping trying	Making links
Being willing to 'have a go'	Enjoying what they set out to do	Choosing ways to do things

The observation carried out above gives a detailed description of what the practitioner observed the child doing, and each of the areas of learning covered are then highlighted so that the reader can see at a glance which of the prime and specific areas of development have been focused on. The characteristics of effective learning covered in the observed activity are also shown by highlighting.

The observation takes into account what the child can do now whilst focusing on his next steps, enabling the practitioner to plan for future activities.

Integrated review

The integrated review was introduced in September 2015 to bring together the Healthy Child Programme (HCP) health and development review and the EYFS progress check, which was previously used to assess children's development at 24 to 36 months old and identify opportunities for early intervention.

The integrated review was crucially seen as a way for health and early years professionals to 'pool' information and understanding of a child's progress and development at the age of two and allow parents and children themselves to take part in the process.

Typically the two-year progress check done in a nursery setting should coincide with the two-year check carried out by the child's health visitor and any concerns should be shared at that time. Below is an example template for a two-year progress check. A printable version is also available at www.bloomsbury.com/outstanding-nursery-leader.

TWO-YEAR ASSESSMENT (INTEGRATED REVIEW)
Name of child   Date of birth
Current age in months   Gender
Key person
Prime areas of learning
Personal, social and emotional Stage of development
Communication and language Stage of development
Physical Stage of development
Current next steps at nursery
Parent comments
Additional information (other agencies involved, SEN support, etc.)
Signed (Key person)   Date
Signed (Parent)   Date

Planning for a child's development

Children should, wherever possible, be allowed to choose and explore play opportunities themselves in order that they can self-select and initiate their own play and learning. They should be allowed freedom, without interruption, to enjoy play in their own time and in a manner that they choose. It can sometimes be difficult for practitioners to know when to become involved and when to watch, and experience will definitely be beneficial when making these kinds of decisions. Children can often be self-conscious but, when engrossed in play, they lose these feelings and can often be observed in a completely different light. It is during these times that practitioners should participate in a child's play only when they are invited to do so by the child or children or if a situation should arise whereby a child may be in danger either physically or emotionally.

It is, when considering the role of the practitioner in play, a time when we are probably best exploring some of the pioneers whose work has contributed hugely to how practitioners, past and present, work with children and young people. Some of these pioneers, whose work is hugely respected, include:

- Friedrich Froebel – 1782–1852
- Maria Montessori – 1870–1952
- Rudolf Steiner – 1861–1925
- Margaret McMillan – 1860–1931
- Susan Isaacs – 1885–1948

The aforementioned pioneers vary enormously in their work, from the belief of Maria Montessori that play was rather pointless for young children and that encouraging children to have their own ideas before working through her graded learning sequence was not beneficial, to the very different approach of Friedrich Froebel, who invented finger play, songs and rhymes and encouraged children to take part in arts and crafts.

Theories and philosophical approaches
We will now look more closely at some of the pioneers of early years and their approaches to play.

Friedrich Froebel

Froebel was born in 1782 at a time when many believed that some children were born 'evil' and needed harsh discipline and structured education in order to encourage them to be good. Froebel, however, did not support this theory and he believed that all children were essentially born 'good' and that it was their upbringing and environment that moulded them. It was with this in mind that he believed children needed to be loved and nurtured by those around them in order to help them to develop into adults who would be accepted in society. Froebel particularly believed that play was important in helping children learn and develop and he was in favour of children spending as much time as possible outside in the natural environment.

Maria Montessori

Montessori was born in 1870 and trained as a doctor. Initially she worked with children who had learning difficulties and it is through this work that she began to realise how a structured approach to learning benefitted children. This approach was deemed successful when Maria Montessori was invited to work with poor children in Rome in 1907. Her approach is still widely used today, with many settings adopting her approach.

There are three key features of Maria Montessori's approach, and these are:

- Absorbent mind – it was the belief of Maria Montessori that children could learn without effort from birth until the age of six years.

- Time not to be wasted – as Maria Montessori believed that children could learn so much so young, she felt that play was a waste of valuable 'learning' time.

- Active learners – it was Maria Montessori's belief that children were active learners and that they preferred practical tools that could teach children specific skills such as cooking and gardening.

Rudolf Steiner

Steiner was born in 1861 and developed his views on childhood and education around his personal spiritual beliefs. There are a number of key features of Steiner's approach, and these include:

- Link to spirituality – Steiner believed that children are reincarnations.

- Natural materials were best – Steiner strongly believed the need for children to be given time and space to develop and learn at their own pace. It was Steiner's belief that natural materials were far superior to toys and man-made materials.

- Practical skills – Steiner believed that children needed practical skills such as knitting in order to develop. He did not endorse early reading and writing skills as he believed that these skills would prevent the child from thinking for themselves, as they were being exposed to the views of others. Steiner believed that storytelling was essential to child development.

- Role of the adult – Steiner believed that the essential role of the adult was for guidance and that the child should be allowed to discover things for himself.

The McMillan sisters

The McMillan sisters – Margaret and Rachel – passionately campaigned to improve conditions for poor families, and in particular children. Their main aim was to ensure the health of young children but they were also interested in educating young children. The sisters funded a nursery school for children from a poor area of London in 1914 and ensured that much of the time was spent outdoors. They believed that imaginative play was very important and also understood the importance of involving parents.

Susan Isaacs

Isaacs was born in 1885 and she passionately believed that play was important for the development and education of children, and in particular for the specific area of development, emotional and social wellbeing. Isaacs firmly believed that play was a safe way for children to explore their feelings and emotions.

There are many other theorists whose work is still used today, including Janet Moyles, Jean Piaget, Lev Vygotsky and Reggio Emilia.

Many theoretical and philosophical approaches are still widely linked to current practice, such as:

- The importance of the outdoor area – this was first stressed by Froebel.

- Working in partnership with parents and carers – this was introduced by the McMillan sisters.

- Easy accessibility to resources by children – the importance of this was stressed by Montessori.

- The use of natural materials – this was suggested by Steiner.

In everyday current practice, many theoretical and philosophical approaches are used, and this helps to maintain a good balance. Different play opportunities can be provided for children of different ages and from different perspectives. For example, treasure baskets (Steiner) can be introduced to young babies and a country walk can be planned (Froebel) for a child of three years.

It is important to remember that as all children are different, so too are their needs, and it is the role of the practitioner to be aware of, and respect, the individual needs of each child. Whilst some children thoroughly enjoy, and actively request, the participation of an adult during play, other children will visibly shy away from such intervention. It can at times be difficult for practitioners, particularly those working with children who are grouped together according to age rather than interests or similarities, to meet the needs of all the children. Difficult it certainly may be but impossible it is not. The key is to *respect* the child. By showing respect you will not only build on the child's confidence but you will also encourage them to trust you, which will, in turn, develop a starting point that will make it easier for you to provide for the child's intellectual, emotional and physical needs.

There are a number of important issues that practitioners need to remember – what to do and what not to do!

When providing and supporting a child in play, practitioners need to:

- Ensure that the environment is stimulating, exciting and welcoming.

- Ensure that children have access to both the indoor and outdoor areas.

- Provide a good mix of structured and planned activities.
- Support and extend play in order to encourage learning.

When providing and supporting a child in play, practitioners must avoid:

- Having unrealistic expectations of children.
- Restricting children with regard to choice.
- Preventing children from making mistakes.

Practitioners can assist children in play by providing lots of opportunities for them to talk to and interact with adults whilst taking part in interesting and stimulating activities. Research has proved that play is an essential part of a child's learning and promotes all areas of their development.

It is important that the nursery manager carefully considers all theories and philosophical approaches in order to decide where each fits with their nursery's own style and ethos. Managers should take the time to reflect on the vision and values they have for their setting and consider their approach to running the nursery. Think about how you run your nursery. How do you treat staff? How do you present yourself and your setting to those using your service? How do you value children and work at providing the very best for them? By taking the time to reflect on how early years pioneers have shaped current practice, managers can inspire and motivate staff by embracing different theories and approaches.

Child-led and adult-led play

Child-led play has limited adult intervention. The child takes control of the play by choosing what to do, when to do it and how to do it. Child-led play for under twos may consist of activities such as treasure baskets, push-and-pull toys and ride-on toys, teddy bears and dolls. Child-led play for children aged between two and five years may consist of activities such as using skipping ropes, walking on stilts, dressing up and painting.

Adult-led play is where the adult plans and leads the activity. Adult-led play for under twos may take the form of encouraging the child to kick a ball, painting, puppet play and playing 'peek a boo'. Adult-led play for children aged between two and five years may take the form of clay modelling, den building and baking.

Exercise

Spend some time in each of the rooms in your provision and take note of
how many child-initiated activities there are, in contrast to how many are
adult-led. Do you feel the balance is right or is this an area of practice that
needs to be addressed?

Evaluating a planned play opportunity

If we do not take the time to evaluate a planned play opportunity then
there is little point in carrying out the activity in the first place. In order
to plan further opportunities for the children, we need to look at how
we have supported their learning and development in the past and how
we can build on what the child already knows. In order to plan future
opportunities and to improve on our current practice, we need to carefully consider what we do and why we do it.

When evaluating a play opportunity, we need to consider the following
important points:

- Did the children enjoy the activity?
- Were the children motivated during the activity?
- Were the children engaged in the activity?
- How did the children communicate during the activity?
- How did the children behave during the activity?
- Did the children learn anything?

We plan play opportunities to support children's progress within the
areas of learning of the Early Years Foundation Stage. These areas of
learning and development are as follows:

- personal, social and emotional
- physical
- communication and language
- literacy
- mathematics

- understanding the world
- expressive arts and design.

Although we may plan a specific play opportunity to focus on one area of learning, often we can involve children in a number of areas using the same play opportunity. For example, we may set up a role play activity involving a café to encourage communication and language skills, but the taking of orders will involve literacy skills and taking of money and giving of change would link to mathematics.

It is important for practitioners to understand their own role with regard to planned play opportunities. Practitioners need to source suitable tools and resources and prepare the play opportunity in a way that will appeal to children. In order to do this, they need to answer some important questions:

- Have you carried out a suitable risk assessment?
- Do you have the resources needed to carry out the planned play opportunity successfully?
- Are you aware which children will be involved in the activity?
- Are you aware of the children's interests and stages of development?
- Have you decided which area of the EYFS your planned activity will primarily focus on?

Practitioners also need to know how to encourage children to take part in the planned activity. All children are different and some will engage confidently almost immediately, whilst others may take some time to study the activity before joining in. Others may be completely reluctant to take part at all. During a planned play activity, children should be encouraged to communicate, and the practitioner should know what questions to ask and when to ask them and understand how to *listen* to what the children have to say. It is important that practitioners acknowledge what the children are telling them if they are to understand the child's thoughts and ideas. Finally, practitioners need to support children's learning throughout the activity.

One planned play opportunity should lead onto the next. After each planned play opportunity, practitioners need to think about what the child learned and how they can develop. By looking at what the child learned in the first activity, we can plan and support them in their next stages of development. It is important to make sure that children's progress is supported *gradually*, such as by introducing different materials to carry out a similar activity to the one done before. For example, if a child enjoyed painting using a thick paint brush, you can extend this by introducing finer-bristled brushes or other tools for painting, such as sponges, scrapers and rollers.

A good manager will encourage their team to plan suitable activities for children and will be able to ensure that any necessary resources are available for staff to implement these planned activities. Sourcing suitable training and continuing professional development for staff is an essential part of the nursery manager's role to ensure that staff are kept up to date with best practice when deciding on child-led and adult-led activities.

Self-evaluation

Evaluation is a vital part of any business. An outstanding manager will realise the importance of thinking ahead whilst remembering what has happened in the past, and use this information to plan in a meaningful and structured way. The manager not only has to evaluate the nursery business on a whole but they will also need to evaluate themselves, and the role they play, in order to continually move forward with the business's best interests at heart. You will need to consider:

- The everyday tasks you perform.
- The successes and failures you have experienced.
- Any areas of professional development you need to improve on.

Chapter 7
Sustainability

Whilst it is not necessarily the job of the nursery manager to be responsible for the sustainability of the provision, it is in everyone's interests if the manager has the foresight to look at the whole picture and knows how to lead the team to a successful future. Sustainability is essential. If the provision is not making a profit and is not sustainable, the chances are high that it will eventually close, leading to job losses and uncertainty for the children and families using the service.

An outstanding manager will know their market and understand the issues faced by families in their area and the service that local users are looking for. A manager who constantly receives telephone calls and shows prospective parents or carers around the provision but fails to secure bookings will be unable to sustain the business for the long term. Failure to adapt to changes in the industry and to monitor capacity will also lead to a business that is unsustainable.

Managers must listen to what is being asked of them and, if necessary, make changes to adapt to current trends. A nursery who operates from 8am until 5.30pm, for example, but finds itself losing business because parents and carers need to drop off at 7.30am and collect at 6pm will need to review its opening times to take into account the earlier drop-offs and later collections. Many parents and carers travel long distances to work and they may have to negotiate busy traffic, so having the option of using a nursery with longer opening times is appealing.

Likewise, some parents may require term-time-only childcare; perhaps they are teachers themselves or are accessing the free, term-time-only funding, and this is something that the manager may need to address. Unlike simply changing opening times, it is not an easy decision to make with regard to term-time-only places. You may get more business by offering term-time-only places but this needs to be carefully monitored and offset by charges currently in place. Will the provision be overstaffed during school holidays, for example, when the decrease in children attending could be very high? Is the provision able to recruit term-time-only staff to offset the drop in fees from children attending term time only?

Carrying out market research

It is always a good idea to know the market you are targeting, what your target audience is looking for and how you can provide this. It is probably safe to say that parents, whilst looking for a good provider, are also looking closely at costs and the cost, of a provision will probably be high up on most parents' agenda when making the final decision as to where to enrol their child. Although providers want to secure customers and run at high capacity, this has to be done with careful thought. A full nursery, charging too little, will quickly become unsustainable, and a nursery pitching prices too high, whatever they have on offer, will fail to attract customers. An outstanding nursery will know how to provide an excellent service at an affordable price, appealing to customers living locally and those travelling through the area on their way to work.

Calculating profitability

A nursery manager should be aware of the basics with regard to the nursery's profitability and this can only be achieved by understanding the occupancy levels of the nursery along with its expenditure.

By developing a simple spreadsheet and inputting essential data, such as the cost charged per day, the number of days the nursery is open per year and its current occupancy, it is easy to see how much money the setting is generating per annum. Offset this figure against expenditure, such as rent, rates, wages, consumables and so forth, and you will have a profit figure for the nursery. Looking at the example below, we can see that a nursery that has places for 67 children running at 70 per cent occupancy and charging £44 per day generates an annual income of

£526,218.00; however, after taking into account costs and expenditures, the profit for the year is £98,718.00.

Cost per child	Days per year	Yearly fee	Occupancy	No. of places
£44	255	£11,220.00	70%	67
Liability	**Cost**			
Rent	£45,000.00			
Rates	£22,500.00			
Wages	£305,000.00			
Consumables	£40,000.00			**Income**
Energy	£10,000.00			£526,218.00
Miscellaneous	£5,000.00			
TOTAL	£427,500.00			

By simply changing the figures in the fee box and occupancy levels, it is easy to understand how a nursery can fluctuate and why it is important to keep abreast of outgoings and expenditure.

For example, if the setting decided to increase their daily rate to £45 but the number of children dropped to 58 per cent, the picture would be very different, as the nursery would only be making a profit of £18,418.50 per annum. An unexpected expenditure, such as a broken boiler, could put the business into negative figures. Despite the increase in daily rates, the drop in occupancy levels would have a huge impact on the nursery and it is the manager's job to anticipate a drop in occupancy levels and prepare in advance. Spending, for example, would need to be reined in and the manager would need to look closely at the allocated budgets, making sure that the expenditure for the nursery reflects the new occupancy levels. The cook, for example, may continue to order the same amount of food simply because this has become a habit, and the manager will need to carefully monitor wastage in order to ensure the sustainability of the business.

Cost per child	Days per year	Yearly fee	Occupancy	No. of places
£45	255	£11,475.00	58%	67
Liability	**Cost**			
Rent	£45,000.00			
Rates	£22,500.00			
Wages	£305,000.00			
Consumables	£40,000.00			**Income**
Energy	£10,000.00			£445,918.50
Miscellaneous	£5,000.00			
TOTAL	£427,500.00			

Usually, a large dip in occupancy levels in a nursery can be foreseen. The biggest drop in any nursery occupancy levels will happen in September, when children in the pre-school room leave to go to mainstream school. If the nursery is aware of the number of children leaving from an early stage, and it should be, then this loss of occupancy can be catered for and dealt with through effective advertising to fill the spaces and an accounts management system that successfully realises the drop in numbers and the effect this will have on income and profit.

Exercise

Create a spreadsheet similar to that above and (1) insert the current number of children and price per session along with known expenditure, and (2) insert the desired number of children to enable the nursery to make a good profit. This will give you an idea of where things are financially and how you need to move forward to increase sustainability.

Staffing is the obvious large expense that will have to be looked at when a large drop in numbers is experienced, and this is where effective contracts have their place. Staff redundancies are never good but they may be necessary if the occupancy numbers drop dramatically with few new enrolments. By having a plan in place each year to secure new business, to take the place of children leaving to go to school, along with the implementation of staff contracts that allow for short, fixed-term contracts and temporary contracts, the problem can be resolved.

An outstanding manager is always one step ahead and will know for months in advance how many children are due to go to school in September and how many vacancies they will need to fill in order for the business to operate within profit and for jobs to be safe. It is inevitable that there will be some time between the children leaving to go to school and numbers being back to a high occupancy level, as the school leavers will go in August or September, with new starters beginning over longer periods of time; however, the manager will be aware of this and plan the budgets accordingly.

Advertising vacancies

The outstanding manager will know that the right time to advertise child vacancies is not when the situation is in dire straits and redundancies are on the horizon but well in advance, allowing time for vacancies to fill before children leave. For advertising to work effectively it needs to be continuous, enabling the setting to remain on the radar at all times, and not be seen as a 'quick fix' to fill places.

There are a number of ways that nurseries can advertise, some more effective than others, and it is important to look at each method carefully, weighing up the advantages and disadvantages, including target audience and costs. Some of the main forms of advertising include the following:

- Online sites such as daynurseries.co.uk will allow a basic listing free of charge, with features and premium listings attracting a fee.

- Billboards and signage outside local businesses can often be negotiated on an annual contract and can attract business from passing trade if situated in the right place.

- Local schools can be a useful form of advertising. You will have to build up a good relationship with your local schools before

they are likely to recommend your services to their parents but
working in partnership with other professionals and settings is
a vital part of a nursery manager's job so this shouldn't be too
difficult. It is worth asking if you can put leaflets in children's
school bags and place posters in the school's reception area.

- Websites are an excellent way of advertising and lots of information
  can be provided through photographs and carefully worded text.

- Facebook advertising is another excellent way of advertising.
  Although it can be expensive, it can also be tailored and aimed at
  a specific audience, for example within a set radius of your nursery
  or at people of a certain age with young families, ensuring that
  your advertising is reaching your chosen target audience.

- Newspapers are becoming more and more outdated, with
  many people choosing to get the latest news online and using
  search engines to find products and services rather than buying
  a newspaper. However, some newspapers run specific features
  aimed at school leavers, new school terms, school examination
  results and so on, and these can be good times to place an
  advert, as the target audience will be families.

- Leaflet drops are another good way of getting your name
  around in the local area and can be particularly useful for newly
  opened settings that want to target their surrounding area.
  Again, by targeting 'family-sized' homes in your area you can
  be certain to reach a high percentage of people likely to use or
  recommend your setting.

Promoting the business

Promotion covers all areas of marketing and it is probably the most
intangible area of expenditure the business will sustain. Whilst it is
important to promote the nursery and all it has to offer, it is equally
important to know when and how to promote your services in order
to avoid wasted capital and ineffective marketing. It is probably true to
say that some money spent on advertising will be wasted. You may, for

example, be targeting a wide audience and only a small proportion of this audience will be interested in your business. However, by realising that not all promotion is advantageous and by limiting advertising to tried-and-trusted ways, you will be able to minimise expenditure and capitalise on the advertising you do undertake.

Nurseries have notoriously tight budgets and therefore any money put aside for marketing needs to be spent wisely. You will need to decide on a method of advertising that will target the biggest audience most likely to use your service. Whilst advertising does not always generate bookings directly, it will raise awareness of your service and initiate a response.

When deciding how to promote the nursery, you need to ask yourself several questions:

- What type of parent are you trying to attract?
- Are you trying to fill vacancies for all ages or selected ages depending on the occupancy available?
- Are you targeting parents who can access free funding?
- Are you looking to fill the nursery with children from the local area only?

You then need to put yourself in the shoes of a parent and consider the things they will be looking for. What is your nursery's unique selling point? What puts your nursery above all others?

It has to be said that the most effective way of advertising any business, and childcare is certainly no exception, is through word of mouth. Previous and current parents are your best form of advertising and it is important to keep in touch with them even when they move on. Consider asking parents to post online reviews of your nursery on your own website, Facebook or other online forums, which will help to promote your services.

Measuring the results of advertising

Although it is not always easy to accurately measure the results of an advertising campaign, it is always worthwhile attempting to understand the interest generated through any particular advertising effort and weigh this up against the cost in order to avoid repeating any wasted effort or money. By measuring the results of your advertising against cost and enquiries, you will be able to ascertain which enquiries are likely to generate bookings and therefore whether the advertising has been successful or a waste of money.

The table below shows an example of how the results of advertising can be measured.

	Newspaper advertising	Leaflet drop	Facebook advertising	Word of mouth
Cost	£395	£400	£500	£0
No. of enquiries generated	40	25	75	20
Cost per enquiry	£9.88	£16	£6.66	£0
No. of bookings generated	4	8	25	4
Cost per booking	£98.75	£50	£20	£0

The table clearly shows the cost of the campaign, the number of enquiries it has generated and the number of bookings confirmed.

Monitoring capacity and remaining full

Whilst it is relatively easy to monitor a nursery's capacity when occupancy levels are low, it can get trickier when spaces are quickly filling up or when enrolments are being taken prior to school-aged children leaving and, as the nursery manager, you will need to have a clear and robust system in place to monitor exactly how many children are enrolled, how many vacancies you have and when any new enrolments are due to start. Never be tempted to enrol a child earlier if the vacancy has not become free and always check with parents when their child's final date with you will be. It is easy to assume that all children will leave your setting in time for the new school term but in actual fact most schools have a staggered intake over a period of two to three weeks, and it may be that you have filled a child's place on 4 September when in fact they are not due to start school until 14 September and may therefore require a place with you until that date. Never be fearful of losing business in this way or be tempted to enrol the new starter too early unless you have a *current* space available.

It is useful to have a database in place that logs each room, how many children can be housed in the room and how many staff are available. That way you can see at a glance how many spaces you have available in each room and whether you have sufficient staff in place.

As previously mentioned, many nurseries experience a lull in September as occupancy levels drop when children leave to go to school, and it can take several months for these numbers to reach desirable levels again. If staff are employed on temporary or flexible contracts, this may be a time when they are given fewer hours to ensure the setting's sustainability over the quiet weeks or months. However, if the nursery can afford to retain the current staff until occupancy levels have increased, this can be a good time for managers to send staff on training courses, which might otherwise be difficult to manage when the nursery has high occupancy levels. It is also an ideal time for staff reflection, supervisions and staff meetings to discuss future plans for the nursery.

Questionnaires and feedback

It has to be said that many people only voice their opinions if they are unhappy with any aspect of the nursery and the care provided, and few offer compliments freely. It is important to put any grievances into per-spective whilst also dealing with any complaints swiftly and effectively.

Not all users of your provision will be happy voicing their opinions, even if this means they decide to withdraw their child from the setting, and it is in cases like this when the manager needs to act quickly. You may not be able to change the parent's mind if they have decided to move their child from your setting but you may be able to provide a satisfactory outcome, which is much more preferable than a disgruntled parent leaving without having their concerns addressed.

One of the easiest ways of finding out what parents, and indeed children, think about the service you provide is to ask them! For the hard-to-reach parents who do not have time to spend discussing things in person or for those parents who may feel uncomfortable making a suggestion or voicing a criticism, it is a good idea to send out questionnaires periodically or to have feedback reports in the reception area, which parents can take away with them, fill in anonymously and post in a box in the nursery. You can then read the feedback and take on board any comments that parents have made. There will be some instances when the suggestions simply cannot be acted upon, such as those wishing you had a bigger car park for busy periods for example; however, there will be many suggestions that can and should be taken seriously.

Questionnaires and feedback reports can be as simple or as detailed as you like and it would be wise for managers to discuss with their team the sort of questions they would like to ask and the feedback they are looking for. You might, for example, like to be really direct with your questions and focus on certain areas of your practice, such as the menus, outdoor area or opportunities for outings, or you might like to make the questions much more open, allowing for free feedback from parents without specific aims in mind. For example, two simple questions might be all you need to ask in order to evaluate your practice and establish what your parents are looking for in terms of the nursery they send their child to:

- What do you feel we do particularly well?
- What do you think we could do in order to improve our service?

Exercise

Create a questionnaire that can be used in your own setting. Remember to think carefully about the aspect or aspects of the nursery that you want to concentrate on before deciding what questions to ask in your questionnaire. It is a good idea to seek the advice of colleagues to ensure that the questionnaire reflects everyone's opinion.

Reviewing the service you provide

Advertising, promotion, questionnaires and feedback are only useful if the manager uses the information derived from such activities in an informative way. It is essential that advertising and any other promotions are monitored for effectiveness and cost-efficiency but it is equally important that all questionnaires and feedback received, whether good or bad, are reviewed and any necessary changes are made. Handing out questionnaires or feedback forms as a box-ticking exercise will be of benefit to no one and will, in fact, be more likely to annoy parents who have taken the time to fill in the form only to be ignored or have their suggestions derided.

You, as the manager, will need to take *all* feedback seriously and act on any problems that might be brought to your attention through such feedback. Admittedly, there shouldn't be any serious complaints received through routine feedback, as these should be brought to your attention through the correct channels, following the setting's policies and procedures, but there may be little 'niggles' that you can, with thought, address.

It has to be said that childcare places, even with government funding, are still expensive and they can account for a large proportion of a parent's monthly income. It is for that reason alone that they can, and should, demand the highest of services. Competition in the childcare industry is high and retaining an outstanding reputation is difficult and ongoing. You can never afford to take your eye off the ball and must always be trying to please your customers and improve on your service, and this can only be done by asking for feedback and *listening* to that feedback.

Changes are inevitable. They are a necessary component of any man-agement and managers need to ensure that the service they provide is parent-based and flexible, providing the highest possible standards for the children in their care. There are a number of reasons why changes may need to occur such as:

- Review of government legislation and standards regulating the service.

- Realisation that a particular policy or procedure is not working or has been deemed unnecessary.

- A complaint from a parent that has generated a review of a certain aspect of the service.

- A new procedure that has been put into place.

The above list is not, of course, exhaustive and changes can come about for many reasons. Sometimes changes are inevitable and sometimes they are planned after careful thought.

Unfortunately not everyone will see change as being beneficial and some, usually older, members of the team, who may be a little stuck in their ways, may fight against change. An outstanding manager will be aware of this and tackle any issues directly. Those adverse to change may not be trying to be awkward or difficult; they may simply be confused or concerned and it is the manager's job to reassure the doubters and help them to come to terms with necessary changes.

Unless a change is completely necessary, such as a requirement from Ofsted following an inspection, then managers would be advised to introduce changes slowly. Introducing change on a whim, without discussion and prior planning, can be disastrous and this type of change should be avoided at all costs. Non-urgent changes should be brought in slowly after discussion with the whole team so that everyone is aware of what the changes will be and why they are necessary. Staff should be encouraged to give their views of any changes before they are implemented and, if possible, a 'test' should be implemented to ensure that the changes will be beneficial. My own experience of a costly and ineffective change was when I was badly advised to change the way the nursery staff in my settings produced the children's development files. Although parents loved the files and staff understood how to monitor children's development and could accurately assess their progress, I was advised to introduce a new system, which, despite reducing the amount of time staff spent on the files, made the whole system less effective. The advice was given to me with all good intentions and came from someone with impeccable knowledge of how nurseries work but, in our case, the change proved costly and ineffective and we have since gone back to our 'old' way of producing the files. The mistake could have been avoided if I had:

- Discussed the proposals in detail with management and staff.

- Launched a pilot to introduce a small selection of the new files and monitored them closely to see if they worked as well as the current ones.

- Decided whether the changes would really be beneficial to *everyone* (saving time and less paperwork were attractive outcomes but didn't really mean that much when the files were more difficult to manage).

Despite years of experience and running 'outstanding' settings, I still wasn't infallible when it came to implementing change and that is why I would always advocate taking your time and considering every aspect before implementing unnecessary changes, as they may not always be worth the effort.

Chapter 8
Promoting health and wellbeing through physical and nutrition co-ordination (PANCO)

The Statutory Framework for the Early Years Foundation Stage (Department for Education, 2017) clearly states that physical development 'involves providing opportunities for young children to be active and interactive, and to develop their co-ordination, control and movement. Children must also be helped to understand the importance of physical activity, and to make healthy choices in relation to food.'

Physical activity

The Chief Medical Office has published guidance on physical activity that providers may like to refer to in order to ensure their setting is providing sufficient opportunity for all the children in their care to exercise. It covers examples of physical exercise for children under five who are not yet walking (tummy time and floor- and water-based activities) and those under five who are capable of walking (climbing, walking and skipping), together with guidelines for children over the age of five years and young people. The guidance can be downloaded from www.gov.uk/government/publications/uk-physical-activity-guidelines.

It is very important for children to have some form of exercise every day. Physical activity helps children to develop strength and to become mentally alert and stay healthy.

In today's society, when the lifestyles of many children allow for far less opportunity for physical exercise than in the past, it is vital that nursery leaders recognise the need to plan for physical activity in their setting. Not so very long ago most children had to walk to and from school, but nowadays, the majority of children travel by car or bus to school, eliminating this chance for exercise.

Exercise in the early years should be fun and enjoyable. Children need space to run, stretch and explore and, whilst space can sometimes be limited indoors, gardens, parks and playgrounds can provide excellent opportunities for children to exercise outside. Outdoor play and exercise should be encouraged all year round and can be enjoyed whatever the weather, providing children are dressed appropriately.

Physical exercise benefits children in a number of ways:

- It improves balance.
- It improves co-ordination.
- It improves flexibility.
- It strengthens muscles.
- It strengthens joints.
- It improves appetite.
- It increases bone density.
- It increases blood circulation.
- It develops strength and stamina.
- It develops lung capacity.
- It helps the digestive process.

All of these benefits give the child a feeling of wellbeing and also encourage interaction and co-operation.

It is important that practitioners make sure that children are aware of the effects that exercise can have on the body and that they are prepared to set aside times for rest during activities. This can be a good opportunity to talk to the children about how they feel before, during and after a vigorous exercise routine.

Encouraging children to understand the importance of regular exercise and how it benefits the body will help them to develop positive attitudes towards a sensible fitness routine.

When we talk about physical development, we automatically think of exercise and outdoor play, but 'physical' exercise covers much more than just gross motor skills. Physical development covers the whole of the body and exercise is about how children learn to control every part of their body, including:

- **Gross motor skills** – movements that involve the arms and legs such as throwing and kicking a ball.

- **Fine motor skills** – small movements involving the whole of the hand such as catching a ball. Fine manipulative skills may also fall into this category and these involve controlling a pencil when learning to write or draw.

- **Co-ordination skills** – this involves the ability to combine two or more skills at the same time. Co-ordinating the eye and foot, for example, whilst negotiating stairs or using the hand and eye when building bricks or threading beads.

- **Balance** – closely linked with co-ordination. Children learn how to control their bodies whilst riding a bike, for example, or walking in a straight line.

- **Locomotive skills** – these skills involve controlling how the child runs, jumps and walks.

It is absolutely vital that children enjoy exercise. Expecting too much from them at the start or pushing them too far may put them off exercise and could potentially damage their opinion of exercise in the long term. Allowing children to explore at their own pace and to do only what they are happy and confident doing will help them to build on their confidence and skills. Practitioners should avoid over-encouragement and must never 'goad' children into trying something they are not ready for, as, in addition to this being dangerous, they may lose confidence if they are unable to carry out a certain task. As a manager, you need to be confident that your team understands the importance of daily exercise and how this can be achieved effectively using the space available.

It is probably true to say that the most vigorous activity will take place outdoors and free flow from the indoors to the outdoors should be encouraged whenever possible. However, free flow is not always an option for settings and it is important that we encourage both gross and fine motor skills indoors as well as out. It should be relatively easy for most settings to be able to incorporate indoor physical play, which can take the form of dancing, for example.

Exercise

Think about the available outdoor space at your own setting. Is free-flow access available? If not, how do you monitor the time children spend outside? If outdoor space on site is limited, how do you ensure that children have access to other outdoor facilities or areas and how is exercise promoted effectively? Are there other factors that you need to consider such as the setting being located in a residential area where noise may be a problem for neighbours?

Physical activity should be encouraged from birth and the time spent being sedentary should be minimised for children under five, taking into account the physical and mental capabilities of the child.

Diet and nutrition

The role of the physical activity and nutrition co-ordinator (PANCO) works in much the same way as a SENCO and is intended as a key strategy to address overweight and obesity in young children. You should consider hiring a PANCO or training an existing member of staff to be a PANCO in your setting.

Encouraging children to lead a healthy lifestyle is very important. By instilling the importance of being healthy from a young age we can help to combat obesity and encourage children to take responsibility for their own, healthy lifestyles. Learning about healthy eating and exercise early on in life should help children to make the right choices and understand why these choices are necessary for their long-term health.

Children are often naturally interested in their own bodies. They are curious about how their bodies work, how the heart beats, what the lungs are for and how their muscles work. By encouraging children to develop this interest and curiosity it will be easier to explain to them why a healthy lifestyle, i.e. a balanced diet, fresh air and exercise, is important.

Firstly, children need to learn about healthy eating. Most children enjoy sweets, chocolate and fizzy drinks but we now know that these foods, though nice to eat, do not provide our bodies with any nutritional value, and therefore it is important that sweets and fizzy drinks are kept to a minimum and are offered rarely, perhaps as a treat with parental permission, and they should never be offered regularly in a childcare setting.

Some children are 'fussy eaters' and will moan and complain if they are not given the snacks and sugary foods they desire. However, it is important that we realise that children will only 'crave' these foods for a short time until the body has been weaned off this need for sugar and, by working with parents or carers, practitioners will be able to overcome a child's reliance on sugary foods.

In order to provide children with a healthy diet, everyone in the setting needs to understand what constitutes 'nutritional' food and how they can go about planning and preparing a menu that will both appeal to children and provide them with the necessary nutrients their bodies need.

Managers need to work closely with the nursery chef to plan and implement nutritious meals that are suitable for all the children attending the setting, taking careful consideration of any allergies and intolerances. Managers also need to ensure that staff set a good example at all times and that they are not seen to be eating unhealthy food in front of the children.

Exercise

Get copies of your current nursery menus. Whose input was taken into account when the menus were planned? Were meals planned in accordance with nutritional value, children's preferences, parental input or cost in mind? Do the menus cater for all children including those with religious and dietary needs? Are the menus nutritional and do they offer alternatives for those children who are vegetarian? How often are the menus revised?

The main food groups

Foods are divided into five main groups and, in order to maintain a healthy diet, it is important that we understand the basis of these food groups and know how much food from each of the groups should be consumed.

There are five main food groups. These are:

- **Bread, cereals and potatoes** – this category includes bread, pasta, oats, rice, noodles and breakfast cereals. Every meal offered to children should contain at least one of the food products from this group. Wholemeal bread and brown rice are preferential to white bread and white rice as they contain more vitamins, minerals and fibre.

- **Fruit and vegetables** – this category includes all fruit and vegetables, except potatoes, which are included in the aforementioned food group. The nursery should be aiming to provide children with at least five portions of fruit and vegetables per day. Foods from this category can be fresh, canned or frozen or served as juices. If choosing canned fruit make sure that the nursery chef purchases fruit in their natural juices rather than in syrup, as the syrup contains a high level of sugar. Canned vegetables should be purchased in water rather than brine, which contains a high level of salt. (See page 144 for more on the five-a-day programme.)

- **Meat, fish and pulses** – this category contains all types of meat products, such as burgers and sausages, poultry, fish and eggs. Vegetarians would include soya products and tofu in this category. Lentils and pulses are also included. Nursery menus should be aiming to provide two portions of food from this category per day.

- **Milk and dairy products** – this category includes milk, cheese and yoghurt. For a healthy, balanced diet, the nursery should be aiming to offer children two or three servings from this category per day.

- **Products containing fat and sugar** – this category includes butter, margarine, oil, biscuits, cakes, ice cream, chips and other fried foods, sweets, jam and fizzy drinks. Nursery menus should be aiming to serve only small quantities from this food group on an occasional basis. Many nurseries offer fresh fruit and yoghurt as alternatives to sweet desserts and puddings.

The amount of food that we should consume from each of the main food groups is dependent on several factors including:

- age
- gender
- state of health
- level of physical activity.

Eating too little or too much food from each of the food groups may lead to problems, including malnutrition and obesity.

Although in some cases foods are easy to 'categorise' (for example, milk and cheese are easy to label as dairy products), other foods may be more difficult to recognise and extra care must be taken for children who have allergies or intolerances.

The Eatwell Guide

The Eatwell Guide (page 141) shows how much of what you eat should come from each food group. This plate includes *everything* you eat throughout the day, including all meals and snacks.

Depending on age, the nursery should be aiming to provide the following number of portions per day from each of the above categories:

- Bread, cereals and potatoes – a third of the child's daily intake.
- Fruit and vegetables – a third of the child's daily intake.
- Milk and dairy – two to three portions.
- Meat, fish and pulses – two to three portions.
- Fats and sweets – occasionally.

In recent years we have seen the number of overweight children increase dramatically. Paediatricians and family doctors are frequently having

Figure 8.1 The Eatwell Guide (© Crown Copyright)

to treat children who have developed weight-related problems that were previously only seen in adults. These problems include:

- obesity
- high blood pressure
- high cholesterol.

Children who carry excess weight will also have an increased risk of heart attack and strokes in adulthood. There are, of course, also emotional consequences for a child who is overweight to face as they often have to contend with both social and emotional challenges, such as being teased, ignored, embarrassed and rejected, which may eventually lead to the child developing poor self-esteem and feelings of inadequacy and worthlessness. Overweight children may also be more prone to depression due to the way they are viewed by their peers.

Below are two lists of health problems that are associated with being overweight. The first list covers problems associated with childhood and the second looks at the long-term problems experienced in adult life.

Childhood health problems associated with being overweight:

- asthma and other breathing difficulties
- high blood pressure
- type 2 diabetes
- high cholesterol
- liver disease
- gallstones and gall bladder disease
- depression
- inability to exercise due to breathlessness
- Blount disease – reduced function of the knee joint, which causes pain and discomfort.

Adult (long-term) problems associated with being overweight:

- high blood pressure
- type 2 diabetes

- high cholesterol
- risk of heart attack and stroke
- congestive heart failure
- respiratory problems
- higher risk of certain cancers – for example, colon, breast and prostate
- higher risk of dying suddenly
- fertility problems
- pregnancy problems
- arthritis
- liver disease
- gout
- gallstones and gall bladder disease
- depression.

It is clear to see, from these two lists, the importance of instilling the need for eating healthily and exercising regularly from an early age in order to combat problems in both childhood and later in life, and you and your team can have a huge effect on the way children view diet and exercise if this is taught well in the setting.

An inadequate nutrient intake in children and adults can also cause problems. A person considered as being underweight is someone who is not consuming sufficient nutrients or who is not absorbing enough nutrients in order to maintain a healthy body weight. This may be due to illnesses such as cystic fibrosis or ulcerative colitis. A person who is considered as being underweight because they weigh less than is normal for their height and age may not necessarily be unhealthy. However, many underweight people are not in good health and this may be because of bad dieting habits or through the misuse of slimming aids. One of the main health problems associated with not eating a balanced diet is mal-nutrition. Malnutrition is usually associated with people who do not have access to sufficient amounts of foods or with those people who choose to eat diets that are nutritionally imbalanced, for example fast foods, which contain high levels of fat and salt but few vitamins and minerals. The main effects of malnutrition are:

- a lack of energy
- feeling tired and lethargic
- having wounds that fail to heal or take a long time to heal
- being susceptible to frequent illnesses
- taking a long time to recover from illness
- reduced fertility
- loss of menstrual periods
- skin infections
- anaemia.

In addition to making sure that children eat a healthy diet, managers should also be aware of the eating habits of their staff team, as lethargy and frequent illness can often be the result of a poor diet and this will, of course, have an impact on the nursery.

Good health and five-a-day recommendations

The five-a-day campaign is probably one of the best-known health campaigns in the UK and it is a programme devised by the government to encourage the consumption of fruit and vegetables.

The five-a-day programme has become increasingly popular with children and schools across the country who recognise the importance of eating healthily. Until recently, schools could apply for National Healthy School Status (NHSS) if they met certain criteria under four main themes:

- personal, social and health education (PSHE)
- healthy eating
- physical activity
- emotional health and wellbeing.

As part of the five-a-day campaign, the School Fruit and Vegetable Scheme now makes one free piece of fruit or vegetable available each school day to all children aged between four and six years attending LEA maintained schools.

The five-a-day campaign is, however, not solely targeted at children and it is recommended by nutritionists and doctors that everyone eats five portions of fruit and vegetables each day.

Portion sizes are often an area of confusion but broadly speaking a portion could be the equivalent of:

- 1 medium-sized apple, pear, banana, etc.
- 2 smaller pieces of fruit such as a plum or tangerine
- a handful of grapes or cherry tomatoes
- a bowl of salad
- 1 tablespoon of raisins or sultanas
- 3 heaped tablespoons of peas, beans, etc.

Fruit and vegetables can be eaten fresh, frozen or tinned and may be raw, cooked, pureed, blended, chopped or used as part of an ingredient in a recipe.

Exercise

Does your setting follow the guidance of any local or national incentives with regard to healthy eating and exercise? If not, consider researching incentives with a view to promoting these within your setting and sharing with parents or carers.

Packed lunches

If your setting allows parents to bring a packed lunch for their child then you and your team will need to be sufficiently confident to challenge parents who bring unhealthy food into the setting. Whilst the parent will undoubtedly feel they have control over what their child eats, they need to understand that, whilst in the setting, your healthy eating policy must be followed in order to avoid upsetting other children, who may refuse to eat the unhealthy meal prepared in-house if they witness their peers eating chocolate and sweets.

This type of situation can be handled well if parents and carers are made aware, from the outset, what your policy on healthy food and packed lunches is and by giving them a copy of the nursery's policy promoting healthy eating. Sometimes parents are unaware of what constitutes a healthy meal and they may struggle when preparing a packed lunch for their child. This is when the nursery can help by producing suggestions for packed lunches and signposting parents to useful websites promoting healthy eating and meal ideas.

Allergens

Accurate food labelling is imperative for those with food allergies, who have to be extremely careful about what they eat.

In October 2011, the new regulation for food labelling was published, allowing a three-year transition period to ensure businesses could make the necessary changes to their processes and labelling.

On 13 December 2014, the Food Information Regulation was formally introduced, making it a requirement of all food businesses to provide information about allergenic ingredients used in any food sold or provided. Therefore childcare provisions that provide food must make it clear to those using the service which allergens are used as ingredients in food. The easiest way of doing this in a childcare provision is through the use of clear menus detailing whether any of the allergens are present in the meals cooked.

The 14 major allergens that must be mentioned are:

- celery
- cereals containing gluten
- crustaceans
- eggs
- fish
- lupin
- milk
- molluscs
- mustard
- nuts
- peanuts

- sesame seeds
- soya
- sulphur dioxide (also known as sulphite).

More information about allergen labelling can be found here: www.food.
gov.uk/business-guidance/allergen-labelling

Emotional health and wellbeing

The emotional environment is all about trust. Children who trust their
main carers will become happy and secure and develop the confidence to
explore their surroundings. It is the job of the practitioner to provide for
the child's emotional needs and this can only be done by closely observing
the child and finding out what they like and dislike. Practitioners should
work in close partnership with the child's parents or carers to enable them
to take into account their background, culture and religion in order that
all children can feel valued and welcome in the setting.

Environments should be ever-changing in order to incorporate the
changing needs of children. The interests of children will vary immensely,
and whilst a child might enjoy a particular activity one day, this may
well change frequently and the environment needs to be practical and
easily adaptable in order to respond accordingly. Managers need to work
closely with staff to ensure this is effective.

Children's emotions will develop over many months and they will
need time and encouragement to come to terms with the various feelings
they will experience. Patience and understanding on the part of the practitioner is essential. Children need to build close, loving relationships
with their carers in order for them to feel at ease so that they can openly
discuss and explore their feelings. Whilst it is easy to ask a child how
they are feeling, it is often much harder to listen and respond to them
when they reply. Practitioners need to show sensitivity, caring and
understanding in order to get children to trust them before they will
open up and discuss their feelings and emotions.

Children need to come to terms with their own feelings and emotions
before they can begin to understand the feelings and emotions of others
and often, during this time, they will resort to tantrums. The majority
of tantrums are a result of frustration, usually through a lack of

communication skills. A child who is struggling to be understood may lose their temper and become angry and frustrated, which will inevitably result in a tantrum. Children who are having a tantrum should be given time to calm down. It is not a good idea to confront children who are frustrated. However, once they have calmed down, the opportunity to talk and reflect on the behaviour can be sought.

Emotional development of children from birth to 60 months

Birth to 11 months – Babies will start to develop a smile at around five to six weeks. These smiles will, over the next few months, develop into something more and the baby will eventually start to laugh. Although very young babies are trusting and completely dependent on their carer, they will, at around six to nine months, start to develop feelings of insecurity and, in many cases, they will cry if their main carer is not within sight.

Eight to 20 months – Children between the ages of eight and 20 months prefer the company of the people they know and have begun to trust. Around this age children will be able to differentiate the moods others are in and may even begin to copy them. For example, if they see someone who is upset they may well begin to cry. This is also the age when children start to have likes and dislikes and their own feelings may change often.

16 to 26 months – Children between the ages of 16 and 26 months will have very strong emotions and often these emotions will be difficult for them to deal with, resulting in tantrums and outbursts.

22 to 36 months – By the time a child reaches the age of 22 to 36 months, they will have developed the ability to express themselves. This is usually the age when children start to become uncertain of new situations and may develop a fear of people they are unsure of.

30 to 50 months – At 30 to 50 months emotions may still be problematic for a child and outbursts and tantrums can still be regular occurrences; however, the child should be more adept at understanding their own emotions. They are usually happy to try out new experiences but fear of the unknown can still be present.

40 to 60 months – Usually by the age of 40 to 60 months, a child will be confident at forming friendships and they may well have a number of friends. They should be improving in confidence and be able to concentrate for a reasonable length of time.

The Leuven wellbeing and involvement scale

The Leuven wellbeing and involvement scale is a tool that focuses on two indicators of good-quality early years provision:

- Wellbeing, which refers to feeling at ease, enjoying spontaneity and being void of emotional tension, resulting in good mental health.

- Involvement, which refers to being actively engaged in activities that promote learning and development.

When taken together, the scales give a valuable insight into the overall quality of a setting rather than the actual learning and development of individual children.

A setting that shows consistently low levels of wellbeing or involvement may result in the development of the child being compromised. The higher the levels of wellbeing and involvement, the more likely the child is to achieve well and access a deep level of learning.

Using the assessment of wellbeing and involvement scales is easy. It is effectively a 'scanning' process, whereby children are observed for a very short period of time – approximately two minutes – and a score is given for wellbeing and involvement based on the following scales:

Leuven scale for wellbeing

Level 1 – Extremely low
The child shows signs of discomfort and may be visibly upset (crying). They show no concentration and may be daydreaming or looking sad, frightened or angry. The child is not responsive to the environment and avoids contact. They may behave in an aggressive manner and hurt either themselves or others.
Level 2 – Low
Although the signals may not be as obvious as in level 1, the child will still show signs of uneasiness and have limited concentration. The child will be easily distracted.
Level 3 – Moderate
The child is passive, with neutral facial expressions and posture showing no emotion. Whilst the child may appear to be busy for the whole time, their engagement will be superficial and their attention span short-lived. The child will not be suitably challenged and motivation will be limited.

Level 4 – High
The child is challenged and motivated, although sometimes this may be with superficial attention. The child will show obvious and clear signs of involvement, although these may not be constantly present with the same intensity.

Level 5 – Extremely high
The child will show constant engagement and appear happy, cheerful and motivated. They will show expressions of pleasure and be lively and energetic. Concentration, without interruption, will be evident and the child will show perseverance whilst stretching themselves to their own capacity, showing no signs of stress or tension. The child will be confident and assured.

Source: www.milton-keynes.gov.uk/children-young-people-families/professor-ferre-laevers

Leuven scale for involvement

Level 1 – Extremely low
Simple, repetitive activities, which fail to engage the child. The child will display no sign of energy, be distracted and stare into space.

Level 2 – Low
Although the child may appear engaged for some of the time, their attention will be short-lived and they will be easily distracted.

Level 3 – Moderate
Whilst the child will be busy, the activity will be routine and lack motivational inspiration for the child. The child may make some progress with what they are doing but they will be easily distracted and lack energy.

Level 4 – High
The child will be involved, sometimes intensely, without being distracted.

Level 5 – Extremely high
The child will show concentration, energy and persistence throughout the observed period. The child will be thoroughly involved.

Source: www.milton-keynes.gov.uk/children-young-people-families/professor-ferre-laevers

Whilst even a low level of wellbeing or involvement can become a learning opportunity resulting in higher levels, it is useful for practitioners and managers to observe children on the Leuven scales to ascertain the children's levels of wellbeing and involvement.

It is unrealistic to expect children to operate continually at levels 4 and 5, although anything below these levels will limit children's learning. Levels will fluctuate throughout the day but if children are consistently operating below levels 4 and 5, think about what improvements could be made in your nursery in order to improve children's wellbeing and involvement.

Exercise

Spend some time observing the children in your own setting. Which level of the Leuven scale of wellbeing and involvement are the children you have observed on? Are you happy with the level of wellbeing and involvement being achieved by the children in your setting or do you feel some improvements can be made? Is there a particular age group that you feel needs additional attention?

Chapter 9
Special educational needs and disabilities

The number of children who are now identified with a special or additional educational need is on the rise and it is therefore paramount that settings employ a person who is trained and competent in the role of SENCO (special educational needs co-ordinator). Children with special or additional educational needs must be supported in the same way as all other children, and early years practitioners and managers need to ensure that these children are making significant progress in their learning and development.

Prior to 2002, the Special Needs Code of Practice only applied to children who had reached school age, but all this changed in 2002, when the Revised Code of Practice for Special Educational Needs (2002) was introduced. Further revisions have since been made and the Special Educational Needs and Disability (SEND) Code of Practice 0–25 Years was introduced in September 2014.

In addition, section 3.67 of the Statutory Framework for the Early Years Foundation Stage (Department for Education, 2017) provides specifically for special educational needs, making it a mandatory requirement in all settings to have arrangements in place to support children with SEND.

A SENCO will usually be responsible for the implementation and management of the procedures within the setting that refer to SEND. Many large settings have designated departments for SEND that employ staff specifically to work with children with additional needs who may require extra support.

A SENCO in a mainstream school must, by law, be a qualified teacher, but often those supporting children with SEND will be teaching assistants. The staff supporting the children will take their lead from the designated SENCO, whose job it is to liaise with parents, teachers and other professionals who are involved with the children.

The role of the SENCO in early years settings

It became mandatory for all early years settings to have a designated person to perform the tasks associated with SEND with the introduction in 2002 of the Revised Code of Practice for Special Educational Needs (2002). The role of the SENCO in an early years setting is to:

- Advise and support staff in the setting.
- Collate information about a child's background, including details of SEND.
- Complete and update individual education plans (IEPs) as and when required.
- Support parents and carers of children with SEND.
- Seek the advice of trained professionals when necessary.
- Create and update the setting's SEND policy.
- Oversee the day-to-day implications of the SEND policy.
- Maintain records of all children in the setting who have SEND.

Early intervention of children with SEND was made easier with the introduction in September 2012 of the early years progress check for children at the age of two. This check enables practitioners to pick up on any potential problems and to monitor, assess and support any special educational needs as soon as possible.

As with a school setting, there are different levels of support in an early years setting and these are:

- Action
- Action Plus
- Statement.

Young children with SEND will be supported by one of the levels listed above whilst attending an early years setting.

Area SENCOs, who are appointed by the local education authority, will provide support to the early years SENCO and they will advise on the development of their role and skills, offer advice and give support whilst writing policies and completing the requirements of the SEND Code of Practice.

As with school settings, early years provisions must have, and implement, a policy and have procedures in place to promote the quality of opportunity of children in the setting.

The role of the key person in early years settings

The Statutory Framework for the Early Years Foundation Stage states that 'each child must be assigned a key person' and this is particularly important for children with SEND. The role of the key person is clearly defined in the Statutory Framework for the Early Years Foundation Stage and is therefore mandatory. It is designed to ensure that the individual needs of all children are met:

> Providers must inform parents and/or carers of the name of the key person, and explain their role, when a child starts attending a setting. The key person must help ensure that every child's learning and care is tailored to meet their individual needs. The key person must seek to engage and support parents and/or carers in guiding their child's development at home. They should also help families engage with more specialist support if appropriate. (Department for Education, 2017)

Individual education plan

An individual education plan is often referred to as an IEP and lists a number of educational targets that a child is expected to achieve. The IEP sets out the targets and gives details of how these are to be achieved and measured. IEPs are reviewed depending on the progress of the child but generally this is once a term. An IEP is drawn up by the setting's SENCO and often other professionals will be involved; however, it must be done in partnership with the child's parents. On page 155 is an example of an IEP:

INDIVIDUAL EDUCATION PLAN

CONFIDENTIAL			
Name of setting	Date	Number of IEPs at this stage	
Name of child	DOB	Please circle as appropriate	EYA / EYAP SA- Req
Strengths	Interests	Areas of need	
Targets What we aim to do	Strategies	How parents will help	Monitor and assess – Link EYFS	Progress made
Parent		Next steps	
SENCO			
Key worker			
Other		Date of next review	

The purpose of the individual education plan is to detail individual ways that a child will be supported, for example:

- what support is being provided
- who is providing the support
- how often the support is provided
- the child's targets
- progress checks of the child
- supporting parents to help their child at home.

A printable version of the individual education plan is available at www.bloomsbury.com/outstanding-nursery-leader.

Education, health and care plan

The provisions for SEND in the Children and Families Act 2014, which identified the needs of children and the strategies put in place to meet them, were introduced on 1st September 2014, but they have now been phased out and, in most areas, replaced by the education, health and care (EHC) plan. This brings together a child or young person's education, health and social care needs into a single legal document, which clearly outlines what extra support will be given in order for children to have those needs met. Local authorities were obliged to transfer all children and young people with statements of SEN to EHC plans by 1st April 2018.

EHC plans are available for children and young people up to the age of 25, as long as they remain in some form of education or training. An EHC plan will be put together by the local authority, in consultation with the relevant parties, once a formal assessment has taken place and it is determined that the child or young person does have additional needs.

The local authority will send parents and carers a draft EHC plan where parents and carers are able to see what the plan will potentially contain and what reports have been used in order to put the plan together. It should reflect the various areas where the child has difficulty and what measures are being put into place to support these. Plans will vary widely depending on the needs of children.

Continuing professional development for SENCOs

SENCOs have a duty to train to the desired level required by their post but, in addition to qualifying, it is paramount that they continue with their professional development after they have gained the relevant qualification in order to keep abreast of changes and ensure they are carrying out their duties as a SENCO to the best of their ability. In the ever-changing world of childcare, it is important for SENCOs to access any available resources in the workplace or to arrange their own continuing professional development as and when relevant.

Definition of special educational needs

Children with special educational needs have problems in either one or several areas of learning including:

- behaviour management
- social difficulties – for example, making and maintaining friends
- understanding
- concentrating
- physical needs or impairments.

A child who has any of the aforementioned needs will usually have a support plan of some description in place and this may take the form of an action or statement.

Special educational needs is a legal term that describes the *needs* of a child who has a difficulty or disability that makes learning harder for them than for other children of their age. Around one in five children has special educational needs at some point during their school years.

Children are said to have a learning difficulty if:

- they have a significantly greater difficulty in learning than the majority of children of the same age
- they have a disability which prevents or hinders them from making use of educational facilities of a kind generally provided for children of the same age in schools within the area of the local education authority

- they are under the compulsory school age and fall within one of the definitions above or would do so if special educational provision was not made for them. (Special Education Needs and Disability Review; Ofsted, 2010, www.gov.uk/government/publications/special-educational-needs-and-disability-review)

It is important to remember that a child must not be regarded as having a learning difficulty solely because their home language is different from the language of the setting they attend.

It is probably true to say that disability can have an impact on the outcomes of children and young people; however, the extent of the impact will vary enormously and will depend on the individual circumstances of the disability. Early intervention, such as that brought about through the compulsory two-year check, can reduce the impact of the negative effects of some disabilities on a child, providing suitable support is accessed at an early point. By ensuring that accurate and early assessment of a child is carried out, early intervention can be successful by introducing:

- Additional support – this may take the form of one-to-one care for the child, educational resources and equipment, or financial support.
- Monitoring and evaluation of the disability to reduce or limit the effects on the child.
- Specialist services such as speech and language therapists and educational psychologists.

By ensuring that children can access the support they need, and deserve, the SENCO can have a positive impact on the child's future learning and development.

Types of disabilities or learning difficulties

Disabilities and learning difficulties can take a variety of forms and affect children in different ways depending on the severity of their disability or learning difficulty. The list below looks at some of the more common disabilities and learning difficulties but this is by no means exhaustive.

- attention deficit hyperactivity disorder (ADHD)
- dyslexia
- autism and Asperger syndrome
- giftedness.

We will now look at the above list in more detail.

Attention deficit hyperactivity disorder (ADHD)

Attention deficit hyperactivity disorder (ADHD) is made up of a range of behavioural symptoms, which include an inability to be attentive, hyperactivity and being impulsive. Children who have ADHD have a short attention span, are easily distracted and become restless quickly.

Learning difficulties often go hand in hand with ADHD but the disorder can affect people of all intellectual abilities.

ADHD is often picked up at an early age but is particularly prominent during times of transition such as moving house or starting school. Although it is true to say that many young children find it difficult to sit still for long periods of time and often flit from activity to activity, it is of concern if a child is excessively distracted for their age and level of development or if the distraction impacts on their daily life and learning.

Research has shown that ADHD is more common in boys and that it tends to run in families. ADHD is often picked up in children from the ages of three to seven years and it can be effectively controlled with the use of drugs, most commonly Ritalin, which can calm a sufferer down and help them to concentrate. However, the use of drugs usually comes with side effects.

Dyslexia

Dyslexia is a specific learning difficulty that is common – an estimated four to eight per cent of all school children in England have some form of dyslexia. Dyslexia affects the skills used for reading and spelling and is often called 'word blindness'. Dyslexia can vary enormously from person to person and range from being mild to severe. Despite exhaustive research into this specific learning difficulty, there has been no satisfactory explanation proposed with regard to its actual cause. However, it is thought that people who suffer from dyslexia have a specific malfunction in an area of their brain that processes information. It has been proven that a parent who is dyslexic is 40 to 60 per cent more likely to have a child who will inherit the condition.

Children with dyslexia have difficulties with:

- Verbal memory – this is the sequence of and spelling of written and spoken words. Children with dyslexia may struggle to remember short lists or instructions.

- Verbal processing speed – it can take a child with dyslexia longer to decipher words or text. It can be difficult for them to write down a new word or long number.

Autism and Asperger syndrome

Autism is usually diagnosed quite early but it may take until the child is older for the more severe symptoms to become apparent. Language, social interaction and behaviour are the main areas that people with autism have problems with. Children with Asperger syndrome are more likely to have milder symptoms affecting their social interaction and behaviour and, although language development is not usually affected, those with the syndrome can have difficulty understanding humour or figures of speech and are much more likely to take things 'literally'.

The exact causes of autistic disorder or Asperger syndrome are not known and although many factors have been examined, including environmental, genetic and psychological factors, nothing has been proven. Other rare genetic disorders such as Rett syndrome can cause symptoms of autism but medically this is then termed as 'secondary autistic disorder'.

Giftedness

Although the word is simple in itself to understand, defining the term of 'gifted children' is much more difficult. The initial thought is to class all gifted children as being high academic achievers but, although often demonstrating high levels of aptitude in certain areas such as music or sports, gifted children are not always high academic achievers and have been known to be lonely children who may have trouble forging friendships or may be 'class clowns' intent on being disruptive. This is why gifted children are classed as having special needs, because if their talent is unsupported, and therefore wasted, the child may end up becoming frustrated and bored.

Research by a number of educational psychologists, including Gagne, Renzulli and Tannenbaum, although not entirely in agreement on all aspects of giftedness, appear to agree that gifted children have an above-average ability and are highly creative.

Exercise

Consider what your setting has to offer a child who may be 'gifted'. Do you have staff who are able to meet the needs of higher-achieving children whilst being able to stretch them and retain their interest?

Useful strategies for supporting children with SEND

There are a number of things that practitioners can do to ensure that children with SEND are valued and included in the setting.

Behavioural, social and emotional difficulties

One of the main problems faced by a child who has a special need or a disability is the difficulty in expressing themselves appropriately and communicating their needs adequately. This may be for a number of reasons, for example:

- The child may have delayed or impaired language and communication skills brought about by a disability such as a hearing impairment.
- The child may find it difficult to make themselves understood, perhaps because of a mental disability.

- The child may experience greater feelings of negativity due to anger and frustration brought on by their disability or special need. This may result in more prolific outbursts of anger or temper 'tantrums'.

Speak to the child slowly and firmly, repeating requests as often as necessary. Encourage the child to take part in activities and give lots of praise to boost self-esteem and confidence. Distraction can be an excellent tool and it is a good idea to develop a range of distraction strategies to use in a variety of situations, as these can diffuse situations and bring about calm. When a child learns to communicate effectively, they are more likely to outgrow their tantrums and their outbursts will become less frequent.

Giftedness

There are a number of effective strategies that can be used to help gifted children and enable them to remain focused and supported. These are:

- **Acceleration** – this is when a child is moved up a class, either across the whole of the curriculum or in certain subjects. Although this enables the child to be 'stretched' as far as their ability is concerned, it can have repercussions if the child is physically moved away from peers of their own age and placed with older children. Some schools have got around this problem by allowing the pupil to study advanced material within the same classroom as their peers and this is known as differentiation.

- **Differentiation** – this is when class teachers create or adapt the lesson plan to extend and challenge the more able child. Although this method can be more beneficial to children who wish to remain with peers of their own age whilst studying, it can still create problems if the child feels 'different' or 'excluded' from lessons and this problem can be overcome by careful teacher–pupil matching.

- **Teacher–pupil matching** – this is when teachers match not only the learning styles of children but also their personalities, making it easier for like-minded children to study together.

Whilst the above gives examples of how gifted children can be encouraged in schools, it can be more challenging in a nursery environment when children are separated into 'rooms' rather than 'classes', and there may be fewer opportunities to move the child. Managers will need to work closely with the child's parents or carers and their key worker in the setting to decide on a suitable strategy that will enable the child to be 'stretched' in their gifted area whilst also being encouraged to socialise and play with their peers.

Wherever possible, allow gifted children to work together and provide them with differentiated activities that take into account and challenge their creativity and imagination. Ensure that gifted children are not segregated or made to feel 'different', as this can have a negative impact on their ability to socialise and make friends. Always ensure that the child's social and emotional needs are met in addition to their intellectual ones. Where possible, allow gifted children to use their own initiative and try not to give them too many instructions and direction.

Autism and Asperger syndrome

To ensure children with autism or Asperger syndrome are included in the setting, avoid using lengthy sentences or difficult-to-understand instructions. Keep things short and simple and speak slowly and clearly, repeating instructions as often as necessary. Make use of visual timetables and include pictorial cues to help clarify things. Make sure that set routines are adhered to as much as possible. Children with autism and Asperger syndrome thrive on repetition and need routine. Too many changes at any one time can upset a child with autism or Asperger syndrome. Seek additional support where necessary from professionals, such as speech and language therapists and health visitors.

Dyslexia

Try to position a child with dyslexia close to you or, in the case of a classroom, near the front of the room. Support the child with writing exercises and, where possible, allow them to use a laptop or computer. Seek additional support where necessary from professionals, such as occupational therapists and educational psychologists.

Other children requiring additional support

In addition to children with SEND, there may be other children in your setting who require extra support and, as nursery manager, it is your responsibility to be aware of their needs and what can be done in your setting to support these children.

This may include:

- children with English as an additional language (EAL)
- looked after children (LAC)
- children from travelling communities.

English as an additional language (EAL)

Children should be made to feel that their bilingualism is valued and indeed an advantage. Before labelling a child with having 'language barriers', practitioners need to remember that the child's 'barriers' are due to them speaking another language and not because they cannot speak at all. It can be very confusing for a child in a setting whose first language is not English, particularly if the staff are all or predominantly English-speaking.

Early years practitioners must provide for children whose first language is not English, with opportunities to both develop their home language and teach them to reach a good standard of English during the Early Years Foundation Stage. This can be achieved with effective parent partnerships, whereby practitioners can discuss the child's language skills before reaching any conclusions about language delays.

Looked after children (LAC)

According to the NSPCC, a looked after child is defined as a child who is in the care of the local authority for a period of time longer than 24 hours:

> Legally, this could be when they are: living in accommodation provided by the local authority with the parents' agreement, the subject of an interim or full care order or, in Scotland, a permanence order. (www.nspcc.org.uk/preventing-abuse/child-protection-system/children-in-care/)

Statistics provided by the NSPCC show that 64,397 children in England, Northern Ireland, Scotland and Wales were in care of the local authority in 2016 and over 60 per cent of these due to abuse and neglect. Children who are placed in care are four times more likely to experience mental health difficulties than their peers and, of all the children in care, only a third will return home, with 30 per cent of these returning home within five years of being taken into care.

The proportion of children in England in care due to abuse or neglect has remained constant (between 60 and 62 per cent).The figures in Wales have again remained constant over the past five years (between 65 and 68 per cent). However, both Northern Ireland and Scotland have reported increases, with Northern Ireland now having their highest recorded increase as of 31 March 2016.

It is evident that the life experiences of a child, particularly in the early years, have a significant impact on their development and future progress, and statistics show that looked after children are at greater risk than their peers due to the experiences they have encountered both before and during care.

Children from travelling communities
Travellers have their own distinctive culture and heritage and are often misunderstood and socially excluded. There has been a history of mistrust and suspicion on the part of both the authorities and the travelling communities and it has been difficult for authorities to engage with travellers, which has led to ignorance of issues, leading to children being vulnerable and failing to have their needs met.

Under the Equality Act 2010, Romany Gypsies and Irish Travellers are defined as ethnic groups and are therefore protected from discrimination.

Findings published by the Department for Education (2014) showed that Gypsy, Roma and Traveller (GRT) pupils were amongst the lowest achieving groups of pupils at every key stage of education, so early years settings have much to do in supporting children from this background (www.gov.uk/government/publications/ensuring-roma-children-achieve-in-education).

External support

When a child with any type of additional need is enrolled in your setting, you will need to consider what sort of support you may require from external agencies in order to provide the best care possible for this child. It is essential that a nursery leader works closely with the child's parents or carers and their own staff team in order to provide any additional support a child may need. Initially, a meeting might be arranged with the child, their parent or carer and the child's key worker to ascertain what type of support the child may require, and together a plan can be drawn up. Additional training for staff may be required, for example if the child has any complex health care needs. Alternatively, the child's key worker in your nursery may be asked by an external agency to be part of a wider meeting or assessment concerning the child's welfare.

The following is a list of some of these possible eventualities, but this is by no means exhaustive:

- common assessment framework
- a child in need meeting
- an early help assessment
- child protection plan and child protection register
- working with parents and carers
- working with other professionals.

Let's look at each of these in turn.

The common assessment framework

The common assessment framework (CAF) was designed and introduced to enable effective communication between the various agencies that are involved with children who have special educational needs or other concerns. The CAF is a standardised approach to conducting an assessment of a child's additional needs and deciding how those needs should be met.

Children in need

A child in need is defined under the Children Act 1989 as a child who is unlikely to achieve or maintain a reasonable level of health or development, or whose health and development is likely to be significantly or further impaired, without the provision of services; or a child who is disabled.

A child in need meeting is held when there are concerns about a child that have resulted in a social worker carrying out an assessment.

A child in need meeting will include the family of the child or children, the professionals involved and, if age-appropriate, the child or children themselves. The purpose of the meeting is to share information, identify the needs of those involved and agree on an effective plan to provide for the needs of the individuals being assessed.

The professionals who are often associated with a child in need meeting include the social worker, health professionals such as the GP, the health visitor or school nurse, and the education providers such as the child's key worker in nursery. There will also be a senior social worker present.

Early help assessment

The early help assessment has been created to assist all professionals in supporting children and their families. The assessment tool allows professionals to collate information that can be shared in the best interests of those needing support. Past cases have been reviewed and it has been identified that early support can prevent problems from escalating to the point where statutory intervention becomes necessary. This cannot be done by one individual, however, and therefore the early help assessment tool has been created, whereby information can be gathered and shared from a variety of sources, allowing any situation to be viewed as a whole with all the necessary information being available to everyone concerned. This enables the professionals to have a better picture of the needs of those requiring support from an early onset.

Once completed, the assessment is used to identify how a family can be supported and the kind of support required. The assessment is shared with a variety of professionals along with the family themselves, and a mutually agreed plan of support is put in place.

Child protection plan (CPP) and child protection register (CPR)

The NSPCC's latest report, 'How Safe Are Our Children?' (www.nspcc. org.uk/globalassets/documents/research-reports/how-safe-children-2017-report.pdf) states that the number of children becoming subject to a child protection plan (CPP) or being added to a child protection register (CPR) has increased by 39 per cent (comparing data from 2015/16 with that from 2009/10), with England having the highest percentage and Northern Ireland the lowest.

The latest figures from this report showed that 50,310 children in England were subject to a CPP on 31 March 2016 compared with 2,723 in Scotland, 3,059 in Wales and 2,146 in Northern Ireland.

According to the report, neglect is the most common reason for a child to become subject to a CPP or placed on a CPR in England and Wales. The second most common reason is emotional abuse.

The trend in Northern Ireland, however, differs from England and Wales, and data shows that children in Northern Ireland are more likely to become subject to a CPP or placed on a CPR due to physical abuse, and the same data shows a decrease in the number of children on a CPR due to emotional abuse since 2011/12.

Case conferences in Scotland identified the main reasons for children to be placed on a CPR or subject to a CPP as being substance misuse by parents, domestic abuse, emotional abuse and neglect.

Sometimes, after an initial assessment, a child protection conference will be held and key professionals working with the family, along with family members, will be invited to attend. The purpose of the meeting is to collate evidence from referral and initial assessment to decide whether a child has suffered any significant harm, whether this be in the form of physical, emotional or sexual abuse or neglect. If the evidence shows that the child has been, or may in the future be, at risk then a CPP is put in place.

If a child is made the subject of a CPP, professionals will be involved and invited to monitor the child's health and wellbeing, offer support and services to parents and measure the child's progress once planned outcomes are put in place in the agreed CPP.

A child will be placed on the CPR or become subject to a CPP if they are seen by the authorities to be at continual risk of harm. A CPP and the CPR are, in the main, the same thing and they are used to record ongoing concerns about a child's safety.

The length of time that a child is subject to a CPP or is placed on a CPR indicates how long the authorities are providing them with support as opposed to how long any actual abuse or neglect has been taking place. Once a child is removed from a CPP or CPR, they will be deemed as no longer being at risk of harm and any concerns will have been addressed. Whilst there is no optimal length of time for a child to be subject to either a CPP or CPR, data suggests that there has been a downward trend in the proportion of children who are subject to either for longer than two years in all the UK nations (where data is available).

Northern Ireland shows the highest number of children on a CPR for two years or longer compared with those in England and Scotland.

Working in partnership with parents and carers

The Statutory Framework for the Early Years Foundation Stage (Department for Education, 2017) clearly sets out the information that providers *must* make available to parents and carers, and this includes:

- How the EYFS is being delivered in the setting, and how parents and carers can access more information.

- The range and type of activities and experiences provided for children, the daily routines of the setting, and how parents and carers can share learning at home.

- How the setting supports children with SEND.

- Food and drinks provided for children.

- Details of the provider's policies and procedures, including the procedure to be followed in the event of a parent or carer failing to collect a child at the appointed time, or in the event of a child going missing at, or away from, the setting.

- Staffing in the setting: the name of their child's key person and their role, and a telephone number for parents and carers to contact in an emergency.

It is absolutely vital that providers work in partnership with parents and carers on all levels but even more so when SEND are involved, as the child will have more complex needs, which must be assessed and monitored.

There are a number of key principles of working in partnership that should be applied, namely:

- honesty
- transparency
- trust
- shared goals.

These principles should be applied for all partnerships, including parents, carers and other professionals. When effective partnerships are formed, outcomes for children are improved, duplication is reduced, unnecessary or inappropriate referrals can be avoided and communication and information-sharing can be greatly enhanced, leading to everyone working with the child's best interests at heart and with the child central to all decisions made. It is essential that you and your staff:

- Take the time to discuss the development of a child with their parents or carers and agree on the best way to support them.

- Discuss any concerns about the development of a child with their parents or carers and agree the best way to support them, including introducing specialist advice when needed.

- Carry out ongoing assessments and share these with parents or carers.

Working in partnership with other professionals

There are a number of professionals who may work together to support the learning and development of children, and it is essential that managers of settings understand the importance of working with these professionals in an integrated capacity so that it can be cascaded to the team and built into everyday practice.

Each setting is unique, caring for children from different backgrounds, and therefore managers need to adapt their practice and the way they work in partnership with others to suit the children they are caring for and their families.

Professionals who may work together to support children include:

- managers and practitioners in early years settings
- health visitors and other health professionals
- school nurses
- doctors
- dentists
- social workers
- paediatric dieticians
- early support family services
- portage

- play therapists
- educational psychologists
- voluntary organisations.

Completing forms and applying for funding

Different local authorities will have different forms to complete to apply for funding to cover costs when caring for children with SEND, and each provision will need to make the necessary enquiries through their own local authority in order to ascertain the funding available and the criteria for applying for this funding.

The local offer was introduced in September 2014, when it was made compulsory for all local authorities in England to publish information in one place, which explained the services available locally to families and how these could be accessed.

Each council was expected to include the following information:

- The options available, including expert support for children with SEND.
- The support available to parents to help them to access home learning programmes and portage to assist the development of the child at home.
- Free early education places for children with SEND.
- Support for the child's transition from nursery or childminder to reception class at primary school.
- Guidance on health services available and other local services.
- Guidance on schools.
- Advice on how to access advice from specialist services.

All local authorities must make the above information available both on their website and, if necessary, in printed format.

It is vital that children, young people and parents are involved in developing their local offer as this is the only way councils can be sure that it reflects the needs and aspirations of those accessing the offer, and feedback and consultations are encouraged.

By working closely with your local authority and responding to enquiries from them, you will be able to provide the parents of children with SEND with the knowledge of what they can expect of you and your staff if their child attends your setting. You will be able to confidently write policies and procedures relating to this area of provision and work in partnership with your own SENCO to identify which child needs extra support and how best you can provide this.

15 hours' free childcare

The Department for Education introduced the 15 hours of free childcare per week in September 2010. The free offer was provided for all three- and four-year-old children in England. The offer was extended in 2013 to include two-year-old children from disadvantaged families. The free childcare can be taken in a variety of settings including playgroups, pre-schools, nurseries, children's centres and childminders. The Department for Education allocated some £2.7 billion to local authorities in England in 2015–16 and around 1.5 million children took up the free childcare offer. Local authorities have a legal obligation to ensure that sufficient places for the funded hours are available and the money is distributed to the providers offering the service.

In 2015 the Department for Education outlined plans to increase the free childcare entitlement to some families, doubling it from 15 to 30 hours per week, which is estimated to be worth up to £5,000 per child per year.

In September 2016 eight areas piloted the 30-hour scheme, costing an estimated £13 million. The eight areas that took part in the trial were:

- Wigan
- Staffordshire
- Swindon
- Portsmouth
- Northumberland
- York
- Newham
- Hertfordshire.

The remainder of the country joined the 30-hour scheme in September 2017.

There are certain criteria that need to be met to ensure the eligibility of the family before the 30 hours' free childcare can be confirmed, and these are:

- They earn or expect to earn the equivalent to 16 hours at national minimum or living wage over the coming three months. This equates to £125.28 a week for each parent over 25 years old or £118.08 a week for each parent between 21 and 24 years old and £59.20 a week for apprentices in their first year.

- This applies whether you are in paid employment, self-employed or on a zero-hour contract.

- The parent (and their partner where applicable) should be seeking the free childcare to enable them to work.

- One or both parents are on maternity, paternity, shared parental or adoption leave, or they are on statutory sick leave.

- One parent meets the income criteria and the other is unable to work because they are disabled, have caring responsibilities or have been assessed as having limited capability to work.

- If a parent is in a 'start-up period' (i.e. they are newly self-employed), they do not need to demonstrate that they meet the income criteria for 12 months.

- If one or both parents is a non-EEA national, the parent applying must have recourse to public funds.

A parent will not meet the criteria when:

- Either parent has an income of more than £100,000.

- If one or both parents is a non-EEA national and the parent applying does not have recourse to public funds.

Children who are entitled to receive government funding will be contacted directly by their local authority. Whilst providers cannot claim funding on behalf of a family, they can provide information to parents about how to access funding, and settings should make it clear to families that the nursery accepts funding if they have chosen to do so. More information regarding eligibility can be found by visiting www.gov.uk.

Further reading and resources

Publications

Department for Education (2014), Early Years: Guide to the 0 to 25 SEND
    Code of Practice,
www.gov.uk/government/publications/send-guide-for-early-years-settings

Department for Education (2017), Statutory Framework for the Early Years
    Foundation Stage,
www.foundationyears.org.uk/files/2017/03/EYFS_STATUTORY_
    FRAMEWORK_2017.pdf

Department of Health and Social Care (2011), UK Physical
    Activity Guidelines, www.gov.uk/government/publications/
    uk-physical-activity-guidelines

Food Standards Agency (2017), Allergen Labelling, www.food.gov.uk/
    business-guidance/allergen-labelling

Home Office (2015), Prevent Duty Guidelines, www.gov.uk/government/
    publications/prevent-duty-guidance

National Day Nurseries Association (2017), Observation, Assessment and
    Planning, www.ndna.org.uk/NDNA/Community/myNDNA/Mini_
    Guides/Observation_Assessment_Planning.aspx

Nursery World (2009), Observation, Assessment and Planning in the EYFS,
    www.nurseryworld.co.uk/observation-assessment-planning-guide

UK Government, National Minimum Wage and National Living Wage
    Rates, www.gov.uk/national-minimum-wage-rates

UK Government, Workplace Pensions, www.gov.uk/workplace-pensions

Organisations and websites

British Association for the Study and Prevention of Child Abuse and Neglect
www.baspcan.org.uk

British Nutrition Foundation (BNF)
www.nutrition.org.uk

Child Accident Prevention Trust (CAPT)
www.capt.org.uk

Department for Education (DfE)
www.education.gov.uk

Food Standards Agency
www.food.gov.uk

Mencap
www.mencap.org.uk

National Day Nurseries Association
www.ndna.org.uk

National Society for the Prevention of Cruelty to Children (NSPCC)
www.nspcc.org.uk

Ofsted
www.ofsted.gov.uk

Royal Society for the Prevention of Accidents (RoSPA)
www.rospa.com

Index